The Forgotten Father

By Thomas A. Smail

REFLECTED GLORY

The Forgotten Father

by

Thomas A. Smail

William B. Eerdmans Publishing Co.
Grand Rapids, Mich.

The author and publishers are grateful to SCM Press Ltd. for
permission to reproduce part of the poem 'Who Am I?' from
Bonhoeffer's *Letters and Papers from Prison*.

Copyright © 1980 by Thomas A. Smail
First published 1980 by Hodder and Stoughton Ltd., England
This American edition published 1981 by special arrangement with Hodder
and Stoughton by Wm. B. Eerdmans Publishing Co., 255 Jefferson Ave. S.E.,
Grand Rapids, MI 49503

Library of Congress Cataloging in Publication Data

Smail, Thomas Allan, 1928-
  The forgotten Father.

  Includes index.
  1. God — Fatherhood. I. Title.
BT153.F3S6 1981   231'.1   81-1372
ISBN 0-8028-1879-X   AACR2

$5.95

In Memoriam

D. G. McNair
(1899–1979)

who did not
forget
the FATHER

Contents

Preface

Outward changes in occupation and inward changes in thought often accompany each other in a way that makes which is cause and which effect hard to decide. It has been so with this book. When it was planned, I was Director of Fountain Trust, fully immersed in the promotion of charismatic renewal. While it was being written I was at a point of transition to the work of ministerial training and vocational theology within the Church of England in which I am at present engaged.

There will be those who think they can detect a corresponding withdrawal from the charismatic renewal in the thinking of this book. They will be quite wrong, although if they were to say reappraisal instead of withdrawal, I would not greatly disagree with them. Any movement of spiritual vitality is in constant danger of developing eccentric and centrifugal tendencies, and the present renewal is no exception. Its safeguard, to my mind, is to keep its thinking close to the classical Christian centre, and its living in integral relationship to the whole life of the Church.

While, therefore, I would want to distance myself from the kind of teaching that sees in charismatic experience the main thrust of the New Testament gospel and the answer to every contemporary problem, I would want to maintain more strongly than ever that the only hope of the Church is in new openness to the Holy Spirit who brings us into living contact with the Father and the Son. The charismatic movement as a thing in itself may well be almost over, but the renewal of the Church by the Holy Spirit has only just begun.

In that ongoing renewal our realised relationship to God the Father has a central and decisive part. It is both corrective and constructive, a source of confidence and of courage, of hope and of joy. It is with the prayer that this neglected thrust of the Spirit's activity may come into its own, that this book is written.

It will again be obvious that time and opportunity for reading and responding to the writings of others have been limited, although I have tried to address myself to some of the questions that are at the centre of contemporary debate among Christians. The book is addressed to those who are prepared to think about what they believe and have experienced, but I have tried to avoid technical language which would get in their way. Most of the biblical quotations are from the New International Version.

I am grateful to the Trustees and Executive of Fountain Trust who willingly agreed that I should set aside time to write, to Sylvia Lawton, the Executive Secretary of Fountain Trust who typed the manuscript, even when she had no longer any professional obligation towards me. I am most grateful of all to my wife and family who know from long experience how ill equipped I am to write about fatherhood, except that, like them, I know the love and grace of the heavenly Father who accepts us in Christ just as we are that he might make us again like himself.

Thanks are also due to Mrs Christine Rennie who read the proofs with meticulous care.

The book is dedicated to my father-in-law, D. G. McNair, whose end crowned his living, and whose last days, while this book was being written, brought the Father very near.

St John's College, Nottingham   Autumn 1979

Chapter One

Looking for Father

I never knew my own father; he died when I was too young to realise what I had lost, but I have been discovering slowly ever since. We are all shaped by our lacks as much as by our gifts, for none of us starts complete. I mention my own lack of a father at the outset, because I am aware that it affects the perspective from which I approach the subject of this book – the fatherhood of God.

Personal deprivations of that kind can easily distort our understanding of the Christian gospel by making it say what we want to hear, rather than what God is really saying, but they can also help us to become aware of things in the gospel that without them we would never have grasped. It is where we are most thirsty that we shall be most likely to drink, but also perhaps to be least discriminating about what we drink. One of the functions of theology is to help us to test the quality of the water, to distinguish what is brackish from what is living – and there is theology in this book. But it is the theology of a grown-up little boy, who in middle life became very conscious that he had no father, and who therefore has become exalted and joyful in realising that he has always had a Father God. Whether in the end that leads to distortion or discovery, you must judge.

It is as foolish to generalise about the function of a father in a family as it is about anything else in human relationships. But can one perhaps say that in regard to his sons, he is something of an integrator, a factor making for wholeness in the development of their interests and gifts. Loving mothers tend to cosset and even to capitulate to the inclinations of their sons; fathers, when they fulfil their role as dominant male of the household, confront their sons with their own interests and conscript them into the service of their own needs, so that the young hopeful learns what it means to be involved in what somebody else cares about, and to bow to what somebody else, who has a right to command, decides is to be done. My mother generously financed my buying of books, which was along the line of my inclination, but she did not insist that I should learn to replace the washers on the taps, which was not. The dripping taps proclaim my lack of wholeness in this regard to this day!

Mothers tend to promote the fulfilment of their sons from behind; fathers tend to require the obedience of their sons from above! The first kind of love ministers to the needs of the beloved; the second kind dethrones the one it loves and presses him into its own service. An only son in his mother's house can easily become first and central; in his father's house he is more likely to be kept second and subsidiary. He will have not only a helper behind him, but a norm, a corrective, a protector over him. He will know the safety of being second, of not being the one round whom everything revolves, but of being dependent on somebody else who is "greater than I".

For myself, I have always been a bit of a worrier, far more the pessimist than the optimist, and I have always guessed, without being psychologist enough to prove it, that the lack of a father to look to in the early years has had more than a little to do with it. Thus for me a father means somebody who is able to regulate the life of his children from a centre outside themselves, to pull them towards wholeness, to accustom them to obedience and so to offer them security. I am well aware that the lack of such a father is not the worst thing that can happen; much more harmful is the presence of a father who fails to function as such, who either abdicates in weakness or unconcern or dominates in his own interests without sympathy or understanding for his children.

I know equally well that there are no ideal fathers and that, had my own lived, he would almost certainly have been less than I longed for. But, as Jesus reminds us, fathers can be fallible and faulty and yet know how to give good gifts to their children (Luke 11.13) and I have noticed that those who grow up in homes where father fulfils his function in a reasonably satisfactory way are that much more likely to have an integrated personality, to be able to cope healthily with the claims of authority and to have a confident stance towards life that keeps them from many weakening anxieties and crippling fears.

Along with this personal perspective, there are two others of a more public and objective kind, that make our present study relevant and vital. The first is the present condition of the charismatic renewal in which I have been participant for the last fifteen years, for the last seven as a leader. If I were to diagnose and prescribe for its present ills in a single sentence, I would say that it needs to know the Father. If the medical metaphor suggests a patient in need of healing I would not quarrel with the implication, for that is precisely how I see the present state of the renewal in that part of it I know best, among the Anglican and Protestant churches in Britain. I suspect that the situation in the new independent churches that have sprung from the renewal, in the American denominations, and in the larger but closely related Roman Catholic renewal is not at bottom very different.

If we must be to some extent critical, it must be in a very positive context, for the first thing that has to be said about the charismatic renewal is that through it God has spoken and done a new thing among nearly all kinds of Christians in nearly all parts of the world. For many people, myself among them, it has brought a new and continuing experience of the Holy Spirit – God in the present tense – who acts in here and now eventfulness in the lives of individuals and in the fellowship of his Church, so that things are seen and heard which make it plain that Jesus Christ is not two thousand years away in the past, remote and retired in heaven, or reserved for an apocalyptic future, but lives to keep his promises to all who turn in expectant faith towards him.

As witness to this, lives have been changed, people healed in outward body and inner personality; new gifts have been made available within the Church. There has been a reality of praise, a closeness of fellowship, a taking seriously of God's word by those who had written off its claims, a crumbling of ecclesiastical middle walls of partition, especially between Protestants and Roman Catholics, that has been the wonder and joy of many of us who have shared in it. Here and there the corporate lives of whole churches have begun to be renewed in many different cultural contexts and denominational traditions and we have had at least a glimpse of what can be achieved by Christians who share the *koinonia*, fellowship, togetherness with God and one another that the Spirit can give. All this has happened to the churches at a time of great numerical decline and spiritual dryness. There can be no going back on it, and any criticism must aim at correcting and deepening, not undoing it.

That being said, we have to add in all honesty that what began with such promise has in many cases failed to maintain itself, let alone mature and grow. Many churches that in the early days seemed to be springing into newness of life now look back to that time with a kind of wistful disappointment that by no means denies or renounces what happened, but rather wonders why it has all got so stuck and come to so little. Other churches have come to a corporate expression of renewal under the leadership of a minister, strong in the Spirit, no doubt, but strong in forceful personality also, and have been unable to keep much of it up after his departure. Most common of all is the charismatic minority in a church who have been trying for many years to move the main body of their fellow members towards fulness of life in the Spirit, with little result, and who have become increasingly despondent over their failure.

But even worse than the failure to increase has been the failure to mature. As time has gone on, the renewal has been becoming not less but more dependent on strong leaders offering instant answers. There has been a sorry procession of panacea promises calling people successively to whatever was the fashion of the hour to solve their problems and cure their ills. We have been encouraged to speak in tongues, to have our past explored and our memories healed, to join a community, to have our demons cast out, to praise God for everything and ask him for anything. All these have a basis in scripture, but the oversimplification of the teaching offered and the response required often bespeak the immaturity both of teachers and taught. And since each of these, although it helps some people, inevitably fails to live up to the universal claims made on its behalf, there is left behind a trail of disappointment and disillusionment that depresses the level of faith and expectation.

Further, within the renewal there has been an obsession with personal experience and sometimes even with trivial providences at the expense of the call to evangelise and act amidst the needs of society, which is perhaps understandable in the early stages of a renewal movement but which becomes disconcerting when it continues after many years. As Canon Rex Davis of Lincoln, a sympathetic observer, has put it, he is not very impressed with a God who finds parking spaces for charismatics but is not concerned about the agony of Rhodesia. The places where the renewal has resulted in a church committed to effective evangelism or the service of human need in the name of the compassion of Christ are still distressingly few.

Christian history shows that the mortality rate for young renewal movements is very high. If the above estimate of positive and negative factors is in any measure correct, it is not perhaps unfair to picture the present renewal as having pressed through the vigour of its infancy with its only seeming simplicities, into the ambiguity of its adolescence when all sorts of disturbing and disruptive influences that have been present from the beginning emerge into the open and make the prospect more complicated and perilous than it appeared at the start. Pursuing the analogy and connecting up with the personal perspective from which we set out, may we not say that precisely in the second decade of its life, the renewal needs Father! Precisely at this stage in its development it needs the correction and direction that would be given to it by a concentration on these aspects of the Christian message that gather round the person, nature and work of God the Father.

Within the life of the one Godhead, it is, according to orthodox trinitarian teaching, the Father who is the source of all authority and lordship; the equally divine authority and lordship of Son and Spirit are nevertheless derived from the Father's authority and lordship and exercised, not in self-sufficient autonomy, but in obedience to the Father who is "greater than I" (John 14.28). The strength of Jesus in the wilderness, in an agony of decision about how his messianic power was to be exercised, lay precisely in his awareness of the absolute priority of the will of his Father over everything and everybody else. Man does not live by the satisfaction of his needs, but by listening to and obeying what God says to him (Matthew 4.4). If the exercise of power and the performance of miracles become ends in themselves, they can be manifestations of unbelief and doubt (Matthew 4.7) or of demonic rebellion (Matthew 4.10) rather than of faith. Concern about these things needs to be disciplined by an unswerving loyalty to the will and purpose of God. A renewal in danger of being dominated by the desire of Christians to have their felt spiritual, emotional or physical needs satisfied, or by the pursuit of charismatic power, needs to be converted from its own self-concern to a new obedience to the universal purpose and will of the Father. The renewal will find an expanding significance and life, not within its own internal evolution, but only as it seeks to see what the Father is doing. As it acknowledges and yields to his authority it will be delivered from a false and crippling dependence upon human leaders into which, both on the Catholic and the Protestant side, it has been in danger of falling. The way of deliverance from human authoritarianism is the rediscovery of divine authority. It is when we are most captive to the second that we shall be most free from the first.

Again, the Father is the integrating factor within the Godhead and the gospel. It is his purpose for his whole creation that gives meaning to the coming of the Son and the sending of the Spirit; so to speak, he is the catholic person within the Holy Trinity who gives context and unity to the work of the Son and the manifestations of the Spirit. To know him is to be recalled from what is peripheral to what is central, from what is partial to what is whole. It is sad but not perhaps surprising that the charismatic renewal has not attracted churchgoers who have a minimal spiritual sensitivity and are not concerned for much more than the maintenance of an institution. That it has also failed to speak to many Christians who are manifestly alive in Christ, gives real cause for heartsearching. Often it is because the things that are said about the Spirit, his baptism and gifts in renewal circles seem to these Christians to be so onesided and unrelated to the centralities of the gospel as evangelical faith has grasped it and Catholic tradition understood it, and to God's will for the renewal of the face of the earth, as Christians concerned for the social dimension of salvation have discerned it.

The time has come for the charismatic renewal to recognise quite explicitly that it by no means contains within itself the sum total of God's renewing activity in his Church today and that its own contribution, although God-given and essential, is not complete or adequate in itself. It is a good rule that, if we want a hearing for the part of the whole counsel of God that has come to distinctive expression in us through the Holy Spirit, then we need to be aware of the other parts of that same counsel that by the same Spirit have come to distinctive expression in our Christian brethren. That is merely to acknowledge that we are members of the same body who have essential contributions to make to its upbuilding and outreaching but who need and depend upon the different contributions of its other members.

The more the renewal relates itself to the central things of the gospel, e.g. the person and work of Christ rather than just tongues or healing, the more its contribution becomes recognisable and receivable by the rest of the Church, and the more it is delivered from its own idiosyncrasies and eccentricities. I for my part can see no future for a renewal that withdraws into a charismatic enclave and, by claiming to be the one true manifestation of the kingdom proves itself to be well on the way to becoming a new denomination. It is only a little less dangerous to stay in the churches as an organised self-conscious charismatic party building up strength and practising politics aimed at gaining possession of the central citadels of power. Implicit in both these approaches is an exclusive claim to the Holy Spirit that neither good theology nor experience of the present renewal will bear out.

The wholeness that belongs to God the Father is not one that will allow our various expressions of the faith to segregate themselves from each other either outside or inside the same church. His wholeness will discipline and centre down our various expressions of the faith and make them adjust to each other, when each of them, including the charismatic renewal, is opened up to more of the wholeness of his purposes in Christ. The Father is, according to John 15, the vinedresser who cuts down the exuberant growth of the various branches by reducing them to the point of junction with the vinestock from which they spring. It is the same Father who according to Hebrews 12, disciplines all his true sons with the purpose that "we may share in his holiness" (Hebrews 12.10) which in our present context we may legitimately translate "that we may share in his *wholeness*". The renewal needs this discipline from the Father that recalls us to his authority over us, and shapes us into a wholeness that produces balance alike in inner poise and outward expression and in the mature way we react to others within the body. As we can relate to Father, so we shall live and grow. Thus I see a certain parallel between my own personal pilgrimage and the development of the renewal – and both point towards Father.

There is, however, a third and properly theological perspective that is needed if we are to retain any kind of objectivity in our quest. When I read the paper that later became the basis of *Reflected Glory* to a group of European charismatic leaders, Professor Francis Sullivan SJ, of the Gregorian University in Rome, commented that I had said a great deal about the relationship of the Holy Spirit to the person and work of Christ, but practically nothing about his relationship to the Father, although the latter was as prominent as the former in the text I had been expounding (Acts 2.33) according to which Christ "has received from the Father the promised Holy Spirit and has poured out what you now see and hear". I could only admit the omission and plead that I was not alone in being guilty of it – it was indeed characteristic of the kind of Reformed Christocentric emphasis in which I had been grounded. Indeed when one widens the scope and looks at vital modern Christian movements of any kind, one has to admit that emphasis upon and devotion to the Father has not been a main characteristic of many of them. Evangelicals have been concerned chiefly with Christ the Son, his divine person, his adequate atonement, his real resurrection and have of course not denied, but not made much of the fact that the Son is only the Son because he comes from the Father.

Charismatics on the other hand have often switched the emphasis from the Son to the Spirit as the sovereign source of renewal, power and spiritual gifts and fruit. Of recent years they have more and more sought the origin and meaning of the work of the Spirit in Christ; the Spirit is *his* Spirit because he comes from him, he reflects his presence, love and power in us, and his purpose is to glorify Christ in powerful word and eventful action, which bear witness to him. But, as our Greek Orthodox brethren would be quick to remind us, the ultimate and primary source of the Spirit is not the Son but the Father. The original and universally accepted statement of the Creed of Nicea about the Spirit is that "He proceeds from the Father". If the Western Church then added, in my view rightly, ". . . and from the Son", whatever may be said about the Son needs to be in the wider context of the relationship of both Son and Spirit to the Father, about which so far the charismatic renewal has been almost silent. If we allow I John 1.3 to interpret II Corinthians 13.14 the very definition of the *koinonia*, fellowship, which the Spirit creates is that it is a sharing of life with both the Son and the Father.

To put the same thing another way, we have had in recent years a Jesus movement and a charismatic movement. The one has almost disappeared and the other is threatening to run out of steam, perhaps because each is in a different way inadequate to the gospel, which is basically a Father movement. It is not first a Jesuology (a doctrine about Jesus) or a pneumatology (a doctrine about the Spirit) but it is a theology or even a patrology – a doctrine about God the Father. It starts not with the cross of Jesus or with the gift of the Spirit, but with the Father who so loved the world that he gave his Son in his Spirit. And it achieves its purpose, not when the body of Christ is gloriously renewed in every part without spot or wrinkle (Ephesians 5.27), not even when the enthroned Christ has subdued all his enemies and brought every knee to bow before him (Philippians 2.11), but rather when that same Christ "hands over the kingdom to God the Father, after he has destroyed all dominion, authority and power" (I Corinthians 15.24). "When he has done this, then the Son will himself be made subject to him who put everything under him, so that God may be all in all" (I Corinthians 15.28).

To what that means in detail we shall have to return, but it is enough to note at the moment that, just as the Father is the source of everything both in creation and in redemption, so also he is the goal of everything, and the mission of the Son and of the Spirit is to advance his glory and let him be all in all. I am convinced that it is within this theological context that any authentic renewal, whether of a catholic, evangelical or charismatic kind has to be prepared to understand itself, and that such an understanding is full of practical consequences of the most important kind.

This book is an attempt to explore the fatherhood of God, *theologically* from its place in the gospel, *existentially* in relation to the current renewal in the church and *personally* from the point of view of one whose human need has specially orientated him towards this search for the Father and his family.

It is now perhaps a little more clear in what sense I can justify my title and say that the Father has been "forgotten" – not of course in the sense that he has been doctrinally denied. He has been regularly and ritually confessed, but his being and work as Father has been out of the centre of concern. It is of course true that in recent years there has been a great deal of concentration on the doctrine of God. It has, however, been a mainly *apologetic* concern, about the basis, possibility and meaning of speaking about God at all, rather than a properly *dogmatic* discussion within the Christian family on the basis of shared faith about the nature and character of the God who in Christ has revealed himself to his people as Father, as well as Son and Spirit. The question about God that people have been asking has been *whether* he exists rather than *who* he is.

The Father is in fact "forgotten" today in pretty much the same way in which the Spirit was "forgotten" twenty years ago. To "remember" him is not so much to turn our intellectual interest in a new direction, but is much more like the remembering of the Lord's Supper, where we are summoned to an opening of our hearts, a reorientation of our faith, a personal and corporate restoration of our relationship, so that we realise anew with praise and wonder that in Christ we have, not only forgiveness of sins and the gift of the Spirit, but above all access to the Father. When he who has been in that sense "forgotten" is in that sense "remembered", we are once more in the presence of one of these events and actions of the Holy Spirit that mean radical renewal for God's people. It is in that expectation, and in a perspective that is at once theological, practical and personal that we are called to "know the Father" which, as I John 2.13 makes clear, is a defining qualification of those who are his children.

Since we have begun to speak in trinitarian terms of God as Father, Son and Holy Spirit and shall be so speaking throughout, it is perhaps necessary to give at this point in briefest summary an account of the place we understand the doctrine of the Trinity to occupy in Christian faith and life. What are we saying when we say that the one God is Father, Son and Holy Spirit? There are three answers to that question:—

1 We are speaking of God in a way that arises from and reflects faithfully what God has shown us about himself in his revelation in Christ. The language of trinitarian theology is much

more abstract, complicated and careful than the language of
the New Testament, but the *content* of the doctrine of the
Trinity is only an explication of the New Testament doctrine
of God. We are not here in the realm of philosophical conundrums, but of scriptural truth set out in a way that could define
and defend it against the attacks that were being made upon
it.

In the New Testament, as understood in the mainstream of
Christian tradition, we meet the same God three times. First
of all we meet him in the Father, whom Jesus prayed to and
obeyed, at whose bidding he came, lived, suffered and died,
by whose hand he was raised from the dead. But in Jesus
Christ himself, we encounter the same divine love and power
appearing personally among us as our fellowman. God is
now not only exalted in heaven but made man on earth. The
acts of Jesus are the acts of God, the words of Jesus are the
words of God, the suffering of Jesus is the self-sacrifice of
God, the person of Jesus is the person of God, so that the
confession of the Church echoes the confession of Thomas
(John 20.28) and addresses not the Father in heaven but the
risen human Jesus, "My Lord and my God".

But with Jesus ascended there comes according to his promise *allos Parakletos*, "Another of the same kind of Advocate/
Counsellor". The Holy Spirit who keeps on relating Christians to Christ and the Father, and then to one another, is
himself God, God at work in and among men. He does not
hand us over to another, but in this other he keeps on coming
to us himself.

And these three, the Father, God in glory in heaven, the
Son, God incarnate as man, the Spirit, God indwelling and
empowering the Church and the believer, are not three gods
side by side in uneasy competition with one another. In the
New Testament there is no going back on the basic insight of
Old Testament faith, "Hear, O Israel: the Lord our God is
one Lord" (Deuteronomy 6.4). But this one God lives his life
in three different ways. This is indeed mystery beyond our
understanding, but the point is that it is authentic mystery,
inherent in and essential to the account of God and his nature

and action that the New Testament gospel presents, and not some philosophical puzzle invented by men in their cleverness. It clarifies and reflects the gospel, rather than complicating and obscuring it. The Trinity as made known in the New Testament is often called the *revealed* or *economic* Trinity – the one who speaks and acts in the New Testament *economy* or dispensation.

2 But the doctrine of the Trinity says something that does not go beyond the first point but that underlines and clarifies it. For it adds the claim that as God has revealed himself in Christ, so he is in himself. What he does through his Son on earth reveals what he is like from eternity to eternity. His revelation in the gospel tells us the ultimate truth about God's being and nature, or else it is not authentic revelation at all. The love of the Father sending, empowering, guiding, finally vindicating his Son, the love of the Son, coming, obeying, suffering, dying, are particular historical expressions of the love that eternally flows between Father and Son at the heart of the life of God. The complex of relationships between Father, Son and Spirit are not just the *means* by which God communicates with us, they are an essential part of the content of that communication. They are not just *how* he speaks, but part of *what* he says. If these relationships are not of eternal significance, then the gospel itself is not of eternal significance. That God not only acts in history as Father, Son and Spirit, but that he *is* in himself Father, Son and Spirit is the doctrine of the *immanent* or *essential* Trinity. We note it at the moment and shall return to it later.

3 But the doctrine of the Trinity, besides speaking of God's action (economic Trinity) and God's being (immanent Trinity) has a *regulative* function specially relevant to our present concerns. If the shape of God's historical action in Christ, and the shape of the life of God himself is trinitarian, then the shape of the life of the Church has to be trinitarian as well. In its doctrine, worship, fellowship and witness the Church needs to be related equally and appropriately to the Father,

the Son and the Spirit. The Creator, the Saviour and the Sanctifier, who are yet one, need to operate in their own distinctive ways among us, so that each brings his own distinctive gift in a way that is in right relationship with the other two.

All onesidedness in the faith or practice of the churches can be understood in trinitarian terms as a failure to do due honour to one of the persons of the Trinity, or to realise their proper relationships to one another. Some examples – and I shall try to chose the most relevant – will help to make this clear:—

a The function of the Father is to send the Son and the Spirit, so that he cannot be rightly understood or approached as Creator except through his Son and in his Spirit. God the Father out of the context of the coming of Christ quickly ceases to be Father at all. He quickly becomes instead the remote and distant God of the philosophers, the anonymous and abstract ground of our being, who is in everything in general but never does anything in particular. He becomes the God at the end of an argument, the first cause that was needed to get everything started, the intelligent designer required to account for the purpose and order in the world. As such he becomes a concept or a presupposition, rather than a personal presence and power; he belongs to the debating society rather than the Church, is a subject of interest rather than an object of worship. This is the God of much present day university theology, who is shut up among the conflicting concepts and newest theories and is never allowed to become active and eventful in the ordinary world where people live. The charismatic renewal may be seen as part of a healthy and necessary corrective to all this. There are a million ways in which we can think about God, but only one way in which God has spoken and acted decisively among us – through his Son and in his Spirit. The history of religious philosophy proves the truth of the claim of Jesus, "No one comes to the *Father* except through me" (John 14.6). There is no down to earth God except the God who came down to earth in Christ. So, no Father without the Son and the Spirit.

b But of course there is the opposite extreme in which we over-emphasise our experiences of the Spirit in abstraction from the truth and work of Father and Son. Here the final court of appeal is the vivid religious experience of individuals and groups, where the claim is that the experience is self-validating without reference to anything outside itself. In this realm we are interested in our religious experiences in and for themselves, and the more sensational and satisfying they are, the more likely we are to build a great deal upon them. There is a thirst for miracles and a disinclination to ask in whose name they are being performed; to value techniques of healing without enquiring too carefully about whether their pre-suppositions are in line with the gospel. A recent evidence of this tendency in charismatic circles has been the obsession with such phenomena as falling down in a trance when hands are laid on at meetings, called variously being slain or resting in the Spirit. This has been much sought after and even called "the Blessing" whereas it seems to be clear that it has very little claim to authenticity in terms of the statements and priorities of the New Testament gospel, and to my mind it is largely a *diversion and distraction from spiritual renewal rather than an expression of it*[1].

In the New Testament there is no such autonomous realm of the Spirit, which evolves from inside itself, building on its own experiences and developing its own techniques. The realm of the Spirit is entirely subordinate to that of the Father and the Son. The Spirit does and brings nothing of himself or on his own authority but simply takes the things of Christ and shows them to us (John 16.15), just as the Son also does nothing on his own authority but only what he sees the Father doing (John 5.19). Thus the norm and measure by which the authentic works of the Holy Spirit can be recognised and assessed is that they are reflections and outworkings of the normative action of the Father and the Son described in the gospel. This is precisely the test that John proposes for true prophecy, "This is how you can recognise the Spirit of God: Every spirit that acknowledges that Jesus Christ has come in the flesh is from God, but every spirit that does not acknowledge Jesus is not from God" (I John 4.2–3). Thus spiritual experiences have not to be taken at their face value but are to be judged by what is an almost explicitly trinitarian criterion – the action of the Spirit will always correspond to the action of the Father in the Son – and to the Son come in the flesh, in the human life and action of Jesus of Nazareth which is the subject and centre of the gospel. What stems from that is the work of the Spirit; what does not, is not.

c In contrast to this one-sided over-emphasis upon experience of the Spirit, there is a cross-centred evangelicalism which for good and proper reasons sees the one focal point of God's action in the work of Christ on Calvary. It wants to root our faith on what he did there uniquely, unrepeatedly and alone, and it tends to view with suspicion any work of the Spirit in the believer that goes beyond conviction of sin and conversion as detracting from the completeness of what Christ has done for us.

This tends to be at its strongest in churches of the Lutheran tradition where any emphasis upon the work of the Spirit "in us" is seen to be in latent competition with the work of Christ "for us", to the point that it sometimes seems that the believer magnifies the freeness of God's grace more as a forgiven but unchanged sinner, than as a man in whom the crucified Saviour has worked his regenerating and renewing change. Lutherans are afraid that if anything happens within us, that happening rather than Christ's work will be seen as the basis of our standing with God. It is no accident therefore that the Lutheran state churches of German-speaking Europe and Scandinavia have been among the most resistant to the charismatic renewal.

In less extreme form the same tendency appears where conversion is understood more as a change of belief than as a change of life. My confidence that I am forgiven, a new creature, filled with the Spirit is that the Bible promises those things to Christians and I believe the Bible, apart from whether I have actually experienced any release of conscience, change of life and lifestyle, manifestation of power and love.

But can one really claim New Testament support for a belief in grace that does not change a life lived under law in bondage to all sorts of "oughtage and mustery" (to borrow Cecil Cousen's phrase)? Does the New Testament really teach a justification that does not show itself in the beginnings of sanctification, a reconciliation with God that does not lead to confidence before him and power in his service? Can we really honour the uniquely effective work of the Son on the cross without showing how it is applied to us experientially and eventfully in the gift of the Spirit? The gratuitous undeserved nature of the coming of the Spirit is in fact the most powerful witness to the gratuitous undeserved nature of the work done on Calvary. Far from being in competition with the work of Christ, the work of the Spirit acknowledges it as its source and presents itself as evidence of its effectiveness. The proof that our sins have really been forgiven on the sole initiative of Christ is that at his command and in the power of his Spirit we recover from our paralysis, take up our bed and walk (Mark 2.10–12).

It is good to make this point, but nowadays there is no need to labour it, because there has arisen in recent years a new style evangelicalism that has listened to some of the good things that the charismatic renewal has been saying, so that the old doctrinal and dispensational limitations on the work of the Spirit are in process of being swept away. The contemporary situation, at least in Britain, is one of considerable balance in the understanding of the relationship between the objective work of Christ for us, and the experiential work of the Spirit in us. If evangelicals still tend to stress the former, and charismatics the latter, that is a healthy tension that can only benefit both. There is no work of the Spirit that does not depend upon the work of Jesus on Calvary; there is no gospel of the cross that is not also a promise of the Spirit.

d But as we look to Christ and the Spirit in their togetherness, we dare not forget the Father. If we do we shall see Jesus only as the one who faces in our direction, as Saviour, Healer, Baptiser in the Spirit, Renewer of the Church, who by his

Spirit meets our needs for pardon, wholeness, satisfaction and self-fulfilment. We shall see the value of Jesus as his value to us rather than as his value to God. The charismatic renewal is in danger of becoming imprisoned in just such a man-centred, need-dominated distortion of the gospel where Christ and his Spirit can be easily reduced to the source of our blessings and the satisfiers and servants of our needs.

We shall return to this often, but suffice to say at the moment that the Jesus of the gospels will just not fit into this mould, because it leaves out his chief priority. He was never the servant of the needs that pressed around him; his agenda was not written for him by the insatiable demands of those who thronged him, but rather by his obedience to his heavenly Father. His life was not dominated by the claims of men, but surrendered to the claim of God. To see the place of the Father in the life of Jesus helps us to see that our own greatest need is conversion from an obsession with our needs to an obedience-centred Christianity in which healing is only a prelude to following, being renewed to giving yourself in sacrifice to the one who has renewed you.

Thus we need full orientation to the whole Trinity, to Spirit and Son but also to the Father to remind us that man's chief end is not to have his soul saved, or his body healed or even his church revived – but it is to glorify God and enjoy him for ever. In its best moods that is true of the renewal also, when its worship ceases to be simply religious entertainment or mutual edification and becomes God-centred praise, when in the power of the Spirit a man or a church are delivered from their own problems and are available to serve and suffer as God appoints.

That will happen more and more as the shape of the Christian life in the Spirit becomes the same shape as the New Testament gospel and the life of the God that gave it, and as in the Spirit and through the Son we seek and find the Father. "Lord, show us the Father and that will be enough for us" (John 14.8).

1 For a balanced and discerning discussion of this matter see Cardinal L. J. Suenens' *Ecumenism and Charismatic Renewal: Theological and Pastoral Orientations* (Darton, Longman & Todd 1978) pp 66–67.

Chapter Two

Finding Father

If we look in the New Testament for a connection between the work of the Spirit and our relationship to the Father, we shall find it in the letters of Paul. He mentions more than once two confessional cries which are the immediate result of the operation of the Spirit in the lives of members of the Church. The first is *Kurios Iesous*, Jesus is Lord (I Corinthians 12.3) which, he says, can be meaningfully said only *en pneumati hagio*, in the Holy Spirit: the other is *Abba, ho Pater*, Abba, Father (Romans 8.15) (Galatians 4.6).

These twin confessions describe and define the essential activity of the Spirit in the New Testament; his distribution of gifts and ministries within the body of Christ follow only as consequences. What constitutes the body of Christ is its relationship to and its confession of the Son and the Father, and it is the chief business of the Spirit to create the relationship and prompt the confession. The question whether a Spirit-filled man should speak in tongues, which has aroused so much interest in connection with the charismatic movement, is an issue of quite secondary importance compared with whether such a man is living under the lordship of Jesus and knows God as his Father.

In *Reflected Glory*, I tried to outline the relationship of the work of the Spirit to the lordship of Jesus; here we move on to the other basic confession and ask how that work is related to the fatherhood of God. To speak of two confessions is not quite accurate; it is the first that is confession, the second is doxology. Jesus is Lord is a confession of faith directed towards men and indeed contains within itself the basic norm of all Christian faith and confession. Abba, Father is addressed less to men than to God. It is less an utterance of faith than a cry of praise. We are here in the realm of worship in which we do not so much speak about God as approach him as Father in the access that the Spirit gives us. We shall have occasion to note the praiseful, prayerful and even liturgical character of the New Testament's affirmation of God's fatherhood at many different points. Here theology turns to worship, confession into adoration.

We should also note that the Abba cry is implicitly trinitarian in context and meaning. The very word Abba makes it quite clear that the new name with which we are addressing God is not one of our own choosing or devising, but has its distinctive origin in the language of Jesus who alone spoke of God in this way. To say it after him is to acknowledge that we have learnt it from him, that the right to use it derives from him, and is conferred upon us by the Holy Spirit, who takes what was first in Christ and makes it real for us. Here the Trinity is undivided. We approach the Father and call him Abba through the Son and in the Spirit.

Passing now beyond such general preliminaries to a more detailed analysis of the Abba cry, we need to recognise several distinctive levels on which we must approach it, if we are going to understand its objective meaning as well as its subjective significance for us.

1 It has a *historical location*[1]. In the history and extension of the Christian mission this cry has been uttered in many languages and cultural contexts, but its meaning for us is defined by its use in that particular historical and cultural setting in which God chose to speak his Incarnate Word. Several factors emerge:

a The cry is first uttered in a society whose idea of fatherhood is quite different from and alien to ours. The presupposition, for example, of such a familiar New Testament story as the parable of the prodigal son is that the normal relation of a son to his father is one of lifelong dependence. The elder son in that story does what is expected of all sons, stays in his father's house and proximity, working his farm under his direction, economically dependent on his generosity in order even to give a party to his friends, remaining under his unquestioned authority as long as the old man lives. The younger son sins against that relationship not when he falls into riotous living, but when he seeks independence, takes his goods and leaves his father's house. For us such a departure of a grown son from under the parental roof is a sign of adult maturity. According to Helmut Thielicke, the French writer André Gide has invented "another ending to the parable and has the returned prodigal sending his brother out into the far country so that he too can 'grow up' and 'mature'".[2] Such a contrast in reactions very vividly demonstrates how far we have moved from the patriarchal assumptions within which both Old and New Testaments were written. In that culture the father was absolute disposer and sovereign protector of his children all his life. Before we begin to react to that, we have simply to recognise it, and to see that it was against that background that the doctrine of God's fatherhood was first defined.

I do not believe that the New Testament doctrine is limited and still less invalidated by that fact, but I do believe that it cannot be understood apart from it. Father in the Bible is not the indulgent daddy of the twentieth century, but the one who has authoritative and absolute rights to the obedience of his children. When that paternalistic concept is brought into relationship with the God of Jesus Christ, it is modified and transformed in all sorts of ways. The absolute heavenly Father, both *affirms* and also *relativises* the claim of the earthly father. If our attitude to our parents conditions our attitude to God, it is at least as true that when our attitude to God is purified, redefined and enlivened into new immediacy – as happens when he is known as Abba – that will have even more far reaching effects on our attitude to our earthly parents and our children. One of the promises made to Zechariah about his son John was that he would turn "the hearts of the fathers to their children" (Luke 1.17). To know God as Father makes us different kinds of fathers, conditioned not just by our culture but by our experience of God.

That is, however, to anticipate. Let us simply note for the moment that it was to a society with such patriarchal assumptions that Jesus addressed himself and that what he did not correct or transform in its concept of fatherhood he must be taken to have accepted and affirmed.

b Notice also that Abba is spoken in a religious environment in which father was already one of the basic titles for God. In all kinds of pagan religion, from crude animism to the sophistication of Socratic and Platonic philosophy, long before Jesus religious men spoke of the gods and of God as their father. The *Panpater*, the universal Father, was a familiar figure in the environment of both prophets and apostles.

In all such contexts God's fatherhood affirmed a natural affinity between the divine begetter and his human children. He is our father because he is the ultimate origin of our being in such a way that simply by being men we share his nature. This divine begetting may be understood physically and sexually as in the Greek stories of the *hieroi gamoi*, "holy(!) marriages" between the gods of Olympus and mortal women. A nation or tribe would claim to be the children of a god in the literal sense that their first ancestor had a god for his father. Alternatively in the Philistine pagan religions which Old Testament Israel confronted, the earth mother had to be fertilised every year by the sky father in a context of sexual orgy and sacred prostitution, in order that the land might become fruitful for new harvests.

In the more sophisticated and philosophical approach of Platonists and Stoics such myths and legends were demythologised and interpreted to affirm the basic affinity between the divine and the human. Human reason was man's participation in the divine realm – the *sperma logikon*, the rational seed that owed its origin to the divine. From these Greek beginnings, God's universal fatherhood of all men has been a continuing theme of western philosophy. He is first cause and creative principle who puts something of his own infinite mind into the finite minds of men. Such a theme was taken up into the liberal Protestantism of the nineteenth century, which made the twin pillars of its "gospel" the natural and universal fatherhood of God, and the brotherhood of man which was a consequence of it. Such universal and natural truths were declared to be the timeless essence of the message that Jesus declared.

Such a general, diffuse and philosophically remote notion of God's fatherhood was of course in far greater continuity, as we shall see, with pagan and Hellenistic origins than with Hebrew and Christian traditions. We do need to note, however, that such an alternative notion of universal divine fatherhood predates and accompanies the teaching of Jesus on the subject and is still around today, so that we need to ask very carefully how the teaching of the biblical documents relates to this prevalent religious background of which, in one of its many forms, they were certainly aware.

c Within this tradition of calling God Father stands the Christian prayer to Abba. The fact that the word is Aramaic rather than Greek warns us that it is to be understood from within the Old Testament context of Israel's faith, rather than in terms of the pagan and Greek tradition we have just been describing.

Now the distinctive thing about the Old Testament on this matter is that it is very reticent indeed about speaking of God as Father at all precisely because it wants to distance itself as far as possible from the pagan notion of the god as generative source who has a natural relationship with his people. The Old Testament from the midst of its polemic against the teaching and practices of the prophets and adherents of the Baalim, is at its most austere in speaking of God's fatherhood and almost never does so without careful qualification, for fear of being misinterpreted in these pagan terms. Its sense of the transcendent distance between Creator and creature, between holy Judge and sinful men, made it hesitate to make any use at all of a father concept that could be taken to infer a universal and natural relationship between God and all men or even between God and Israel.

The Jews are the children of Abraham or the children of Israel and only once in Deuteronomy 14.1 is it said, "You are the children of Jahweh, your God", and even here the immediate context shows that they are God's sons because he has freely chosen them and not because of a natural generative relatedness "Out of all the people on the earth Jahweh has chosen you to be his treasured possession" (same verse).

In other words when the Old Testament speaks of the fatherhood of God it is carefully avoiding a natural generative use of the metaphor and affirming instead a social one, according to which the things at the centre of the picture are the free authority of the father over his sons, his covenant responsibility to protect and care for them, and their obligation to trust and obey him. Thus the emphasis is not on affinity of nature, but on choice of will, not on generation but on election, not on natural bond with God but on covenant relationship between his grace and his people's obedience.

Even so the reserve continues. Psalm 103 is prepared to compare the Lord's compassion to that of a father but not to say that he is father, "As a father has compassion on his children, so the Lord has compassion on those who fear him" (103.13). When the king of Israel is said to be begotten by God as his son (Psalm 2.7, 89.27) it is obvious from the context that the reference is not to his natural birth in the past but to his accession to the throne in the present, by which God admits him to a special position in his covenant care and love.

In the Old Testament a father can be said to love his son, but the son's attitude to the father is one of honour and respect, rather than of affection. This is true of human fatherhood, cf the Ten Commandments, "*Honour* your father and your mother" (Exodus 20.12). It is also true of divine fatherhood. In Jeremiah 31.18–20 which may well be the Old Testament original for Jesus' parable of the prodigal son, God's yearning for Ephraim is described in the most tender terms as the compassion of a father for his lost son, but the son on his return is not allowed to say Abba, Father, but only the more austere and respectful "I will return because you are the Lord my God" (31.18). Only in the setting of God's final salvation is that reserve finally broken. In Isaiah 63.16 "You are our Father" is finally articulated on behalf of the nation, in the context of God's redeeming activity towards them. So also in Psalm 89.26 it is promised that among the privileges of the messianic king when he appears in the last days is that "he will call out to me, 'You are my Father'" – as indeed he did, when he came.

Thus, to summarise, it is not in the context of creation and natural relationship but in that of historical election and final redemption that the father/son relationship between God and his people is hesitantly allowed to come to reserved expression within the Old Testament. When the notions of Father and Creator are uncharacteristically brought together in the song of Moses in Deuteronomy 32.6 the thought is of his freedom and authority as Creator which claims his people's obedience rather than of any natural bond between them. Thus the Old Testament begins to define God's fatherhood in a way that is in deliberate and fundamental contradiction with the pagan notions of divine paternity which we sketched earlier. Jesus' use of Abba has all that behind it and can be understood only in relation to it.

d But Abba also has a particular location which focuses and fulfils everything that we have said. We hear it first not on the lips of Christians rejoicing in the new sonship that Christ has opened to them, but on the lips of Jesus in the garden of Gethsemane waiting for his betrayer in the dark shadow of the cross. "Going a little farther, he fell to the ground and prayed that if possible the hour might pass from him. 'Abba, Father', he said, 'everything is possible for you. Take this cup from me. Yet not what I will, but what you will'" (Mark 14.35–36).

i Here indeed the austere context of Old Testament fatherhood has its ultimate affirmation. To be the Son of this Father, to address and relate to him as Abba implies a willingness for his will to the extreme extent of drinking the cup of immeasurable suffering and making the sacrifice of life itself. The special and unique relation of Jesus to his Father about which we shall have to say a great deal by no means implies a privileged exemption from the obligation of obedience which father-hood imposes and sonship accepts. On the contrary, the obedience of the unique Son is a unique obedience greater than that required of any other. As the early Christian hymn quoted by Paul in Philippians put it "obedient to death – even death on a cross" (Philippians 2.8). In its original context Abba means that, or it means nothing.

We must immediately add that the Father whose right to make such a demand is recognised and accepted by his Son in Gethsemane is no stern lawgiver threatening vengeance, and no inevitable fate before whom there is no alternative but to give way. To understand "Not what I will, but what you will" as an enforced surrender is to misunderstand it completely. The Father whom Jesus addresses in the garden is the one that he has known all his life and found to be bountiful in his provision, reliable in his promises and utterly faithful in his love. He can obey the will that sends him to the cross, with hope and expectation because it is the will of Abba whose love has been so proved that it can now be trusted so fully by being obeyed so completely. This is not legal obedience driven by commandment, but trusting response to known love. In Geth-semane the obedience springs from the trust, and therefore in Calvary it is able to rest in that trust again, "Father, into your hands I commit my spirit" (Luke 23.46). God is, in H. H. Farmer's memorable phrase "absolute demand and ultimate succour"[3], and both elements of that description are integral to Jesus' relation to his Father in Gethsemane. When in the Spirit we dare to cry Abba! after Jesus, the one on whom we call is the God of Gethsemane who can ask for anything including ourselves because he has given everything including himself.

ii The utterance of this word in Gethsemane makes it clear beyond doubt that it cannot be understood in a general neutral sense of some natural likeness between the divine and the human, but only within this unique context of the messianic Son setting himself to his unique work of redemption. Here indeed is the fulfilment of Psalm 89 when the anointed Messiah Son nearing the climax of his mission says "My Father" (89.26) and what he means by it must be explained in terms of the unique situation in which he says it.

The will of the Father to which Jesus gives such unconditional obedience is his will for our salvation through the cross of his Son; the final succour of the Father to which Jesus trusts his spirit is the succour that brings resurrection, vindication, new life from the dead. The Father of whom the gospel speaks cannot be defined in terms of any general concept of fatherhood, but always solely in terms of Jesus and his saving work. He is Father because he wills the obedience of Calvary to achieve his saving purposes for his people, and because he raises his Son as the firstborn from the dead. He is known as such first and uniquely by Jesus, and his fatherhood becomes universal not as a natural fact but through the mission of the gospel as Jesus through his Spirit in his Church brings many sons to glory. Jesus does not teach us the general truth that God has always been the Father of everybody, he delivers the good news that God is his Father and wills to be ours also as we are drawn into the very same relationship of obedience and trust that Jesus showed in Gethsemane. The fatherhood of God is not the banal and ultimately boring generality defined by philosophy, it is that which is defined in the death and resurrection of Jesus and revealed by the operation of the Holy Spirit. The "Our Father" is not the prayer of all men, but the prayer of disciples who are following him who said Abba in the garden and on the cross. God's fatherhood is christologically defined and charismatically revealed.

iii The uniqueness of the relationship that Jesus enjoyed with his Father is confirmed by the linguistic novelty of the word that he used to denote it. Abba is not Hebrew, the language of liturgy, but Aramaic, the language of home and everyday life. In this word, if anywhere, we are listening, as J. Jeremias puts it[4], to the *ipsissima vox*, the personal accent of Jesus. His use of the word has no parallel in all Jewish tradition. To quote Jeremias, "It can certainly be said that there is no instance of Abba as an address to God in all the extensive prayer-literature of Judaism, whether in liturgical or in private prayers"[5]. The fact that it is left untranslated at the central point of its utterance in Gethsemane, and also when it is taken up in the Greek-speaking Pauline churches confirms that the very word "is an echo of the prayer of Jesus. Thus we have every reason to suppose that an Abba underlies every instance of *Pater* or *ho Pater* in his words of prayer"[6].

It has often been pointed out that even in Aramaic this is not the formal word for father but is the small child's word that belongs to the intimacies of the family circle. Jeremias tells us, however, that even in the period before the New Testament there is evidence that grown up sons and daughters addressed their father as Abba[7]. We also need to be wary of the suggestion often made by preachers of the more tearjerking variety that the correct translation of Abba is Daddy. Professor C. F. D. Moule puts us right here, "Addressing his heavenly Father with exceptional intimacy, Jesus does not, however, take advantage of this familiarity. He uses the Abba address to offer to God his complete obedience. The intimate word conveys not a casual sort of familiarity but the deepest, most trustful reverence"[8]. In other words Abba is the intimate word of a family circle where that obedient reverence was at the heart of the relationship, whereas Daddy is the familiar word of a family circle from which all thoughts of reverence and obedience have largely disappeared. Moule and Jeremias both agree that the best English translation of Abba is simply Dear Father.

Thus the Abba cry has its historical location within the Old Testament tradition in its sharp distinctiveness from the pagan and philosophical world around it, and is defined decisively by Jesus' use of it in all its theological and linguistic novelty. Only in that context can we begin to understand what it means.

2 But the Abba cry in the New Testament comes out of its historical location into *personal eventfulness* through the ac-

tivity of the Holy Spirit. Abba is not understood by the believer from the outside in terms of its Old Testament and gospel origins, it expresses a prayer that he offers out of an experience of God's fatherhood that he has shared. The Christian is not only a man who has been regenerated by the Spirit or converted to Christ, he is also the man of Romans 8.15 and Galatians 4.6 who cries Abba to God. God's fatherhood is central not only to Christian doctrine but to Christian experience, and when it becomes so, it has limitless consequences in the life of the believer and of the fellowship to which he belongs.

But the realisation of this relationship in the life of every Christian is not automatic. Doctrinally conversion to Christ, eventful infilling by the Spirit and realised relationship with the Father belong together as inseparable aspects of God's salvation. The only Christ there is, is the one who is the way to the Father and the giver of the Spirit. But experientially it is possible to confess Christ and not live in the power of the Spirit or have confidence before the Father. All Christians believe in the fatherhood of God, but not all have entered into the confident trust and willing obedience that belief implies. And they can do so, not by being taught or exhorted but only as a result of a distinctive activity of the Holy Spirit within them. God must send the Spirit of his Son into our hearts crying Abba Father (Galatians 4.6). We look now in outline at some of what this involves, returning to some of the main points in greater detail later on.

a Knowledge of God's fatherhood implies knowledge of our own sonship. When we become confident about who he is, we also become confident about who we are. The Spirit who in Romans 8.15 cries Abba Father is the same Spirit who in that cry witnesses to our spirits about ourselves – that we are the children of God. As Calvin pointed out in the first paragraph of the *Institutes*, knowledge of God is always at its deepest level knowledge of self also. We find out who we are not by introspection or psychological technique but by an existential discovery of our relationship to God. Far more ultimately significant than the content of our subconscious or the influence of our inheritance or environment is the fact that in Christ God has made himself our Father and us his children. For that to come home to us in the power of the Spirit is one of the most healing things that can ever happen to us.

b This discovery is a charismatic gift. To know God's fatherhood and our sonship is not the result of theological expertise or of moral achievement, but a free gift of God the Holy Spirit making real within us what Christ has achieved on our behalf. That is specially clear in Galatians 4.6 where the cry Abba is less our cry spoken by us, than the Spirit's cry witnessing to us, "God has sent the Spirit of his Son into our hearts, crying, 'Abba! Father!'" Before we can say Abba, we need to hear the Spirit saying it in our hearts.

Romans 8.16 reads at first sight rather differently, "The Spirit himself testifies with our spirit (*summarturei to pneumati hemon*) that we are God's children." C. B. Cranfield points out that the verb *summarturein* can mean (a) "witness together with" or (b) "witness to". If (a) is accepted here, then the sense is that "The Holy Spirit and our own human spirit are linked together as witnesses to the fact that we are children of God." "But what standing," asks Cranfield, "has our spirit in this matter? Of itself it surely has no right at all to testify to our being sons of God"[9]. He therefore suggests that we follow the Vulgate at this point and translate "assures our spirit". This is well brought out in the Good News Bible which runs, "God's Spirit joins himself to our spirits to declare that we are God's children," making it clear that our spirit is authentically involved as the locus and recipient of the declaration, but its authority resides in the Holy Spirit. When the Holy Spirit reveals God's fatherhood on the level of our spirit in this way, then it ceases to be dead doctrine that can win at best intellectual assent, but penetrates to the hidden springs of our personality, not merely with emotional warmth but with life-transforming vitality, so that we do not simply know a truth but enter into a conscious relationship with the one whom that truth proclaims.

Out of his relationship to his Father Jesus found the strength and obedience for all his living and dying; to him we have to look for definition of both God's fatherhood and our sonship. But it is the business of the Holy Spirit to take the things of Jesus and open them up to us, so that we in our way become participant in them. That is the basis of all the particular charismata, the gifts of grace. And it is also the basis of this central gift of grace, that the Spirit opens up to us the holy of holies and bids us enter, and become sharers in Jesus' relationship to the Father. At the springs of our being, deeper than emotion or even intellect, although moving and informing both, he cries to us and in our fear and unbelief convinces us that the Father of Jesus is our father too. And as he does it all life begins to change and become new.

c It is therefore not surprising that it is precisely at this point in both Romans and Galatians that Paul begins to speak about the inheritance (*kleronomia*) of the sons who are also heirs (*kleronomoi*). That inheritance is the land of promise, the goal of the whole journey, the object of hope which has begun already to become present and actual in the lives of the heirs who have already begun to enter it.

That inheritance and its various dimensions is described in the rest of Romans 8, but significantly in a single phrase at the end of Romans 8.17, "We are heirs of God and co-heirs with Christ, if indeed we share in his sufferings in order that we may also share in his glory." The heirs will be known because their relationship to the Father and to their fellow-men will be the same as that of the great Fellow-Heir. There will begin to appear in their lives an authentic reflection of the same self-giving obedience, the same grace towards the needy and the sinful, the same persecuting opposition of the world, but also a reflection of the same glory, the same divine acceptance and presence, the same holiness, triumph and resurrection power. The inheritance of Christ is the likeness of Christ, it is to enter into his unique combination of obedience and authority, humility and greatness, weakness and power, suffering and glory, dying and rising, serving and reigning. To define it thus is to expose all cheap charismatic triumphalism which is only interested in a painless and sensational solution to all its problems, as the tawdry counterfeit that it is.

For both Christ and us the charismatic conviction of sonship wrought by the Holy Spirit and the ability to enter that inheritance are intimately connected. It is as Christ is able to relate to and reaffirm Abba in the garden that he is able to go on to Calvary and Easter; it is when we are sure that we are sons that we shall be able to go on and become heirs; i.e. will be able to advance into that maturity of identification with Christ that lets our lives begin to shine with something of the reality of his crucified glory.

In both Galatians 4 and Romans 8 Paul stresses that to be an heir is a consequence of being a son. If we do not know Abba, we shall not know either the sharing of life with Christ to which that knowledge leads. So Galatians 4.7, "So you are no longer a slave, but a son, and *since you are a son, God has made you also an heir.*" And in almost exact parallel Romans 8.17, "Now if we are children, then we are heirs." The location at which we say Abba to God has always something of Gethsemane about it; it is the place where the son comes home to the security of his father's love and knows that he can trust it and all the provisions that it will make for him, but it is also the place where he is called and enabled for a new and costly obedience, where the way ahead is going to have in it something of death and something of glory, till at last there is final death and final glory. That is the inheritance of all God's children. To try to be a child of God and evade the way of obedience is to distort the relationship with the Father to the point of dissolution and destruction; to seek to walk the way of the cross or attain to the glory of God without continued knowledge and dependence upon the love and power of the Father is to court disillusionment and disaster. Only an heir, if first a son; but if a son, then assuredly an heir also.

d When we speak of the sons' inheritance, we are also speaking of their sanctification, because both consist in our sharing the obedience that took Christ to the cross and the impartation of life that raised him from the dead. It is significant that a lack of emphasis upon the Father and an equal lack of emphasis upon sanctification have gone hand in hand in both evangelical and charismatic circles. Evangelicals have tended to major on initiation into the Christian life, to concentrate on its beginnings and to run out of steam when it comes to its growth and maturing by talking of the saved life in legal and moralistic terms, almost as though it were a matter of conformity to rather external standards of ethical conduct, religious practice and evangelistic duty. This means that many evangelical churches, even numerically flourishing ones, resemble the nurseries of which Juan Carlos Ortiz speaks, where the influx of infants increases but few of them ever grow up.

Within renewal circles the situation has not been all that different. The so-called baptism in the Holy Spirit has been rightly seen in terms of effective witness (Acts 1.8), praiseful worship (Ephesians 5.19), caring fellowship (Acts 2.44), and manifestation of gifts within the body (I Corinthians 12.7) that would "equip God's people for work in his service" (Ephesians 4.12). All this has been real rediscovery and sheer gain. The trouble is that in so many individuals and churches it seems to have been arrested almost before it was started. There are glorious exceptions but so few that they can almost be named one by one. In most cases there has been far more teaching and talk about spiritual gifts than effective exercise of them; not many bravely begun experiments in community have got very far; there is a lot of chorus singing that lacks the dimension of worship, and the number of people committed to evangelism and social action remains distressingly small. When one adds to this all the continuing concern for magic wands and instant answers that we have noted already, it is hard to resist the conclusion that the renewal movement has an inbuilt immaturity, and that within the particular emphases that it has made it has failed to find resources for its own growth and deepening.

One is left wondering if it can be because in its desire to see the manifestation of God's life in the Christian and the Church, the renewal has by-passed the New Testament teaching about dying with Christ and being raised to life with him. There are very many people in the charismatic renewal and indeed its leadership, who have indeed come alive to great new possibilities in the power and gifts of the Spirit to whom one would yet have to write in the same terms that Paul wrote to Corinth, "Brothers, I could not address you as spiritual but as worldly – mere infants in Christ. I gave you milk, not solid food, for you were not yet ready for it. Indeed you are still not ready. You are still worldly" (I Corinthians 3.1–3). The church that was strongest in charismatic expression was shortest in holiness – not because there was anything wrong with the former in itself, but simply because it was not an adequate basis for the latter. This renewal has conspicuously lacked what has been at the centre of nearly every movement of new life in the history of the Church, a call for repentance from sin and self to God and holiness, and it is because that has not been basic to its message that it has so far been unable to grow.

But the renewal, like the church in Corinth, is a work of the Holy Spirit and therefore has a great potentiality for correction and recovery. It knows very well that the fulness of the Spirit consists not just in gifts and ministries, but in ethical fruits and graces. It is aware that the likeness of Jesus into which the Spirit wants to bring us is more than a repetition of his signs and wonders, and has at its centre dependence upon and obedience to the Father.

The thesis of this book is that Christian maturity and holiness are not to be found in a narrow pursuit of charismatic experiences and manifestations in and for themselves, but in the existential rediscovery of Abba Father. When we are looking towards the Father, we are not looking back to the beginning of the Christian life at the cross, or outward to its expression in the Spirit, we are rather looking at the goal (*telos*) of the Christian life when the Church and the kingdom and all their members are brought to completion and are ready to be surrendered to the Father. The Father is the God of completeness and wholeness of whom Paul writes to the Thessalonians, "May God himself, the God of peace (*eirene*

= wholeness) sanctify you through and through (*holoteleis* –
to utter completeness). May your whole spirit, soul and body
be kept blameless at the coming of our Lord Jesus Christ. The
one who calls you is faithful and he will do it" (I Thessalonians 5.23–24). The one whose business it is faithfully to call
and bring us to that wholeness, is the one whom in the Spirit
we call Abba, and the same one to whom Jesus directs us in
the same search for completeness, "Be perfect (*teleioi*), therefore, as your heavenly Father is perfect (*teleios*)" (Matthew
5.48). That verse is the crown and completion of the teaching
of the sermon on the mount in which throughout the heavenly
Father is norm and paradigm of Christian perfection.

To be in living relationship with his love is to be trained and
disciplined by it towards perfection. The reality of the Father
will correct the whole practice of religion (Matthew 6.1ff),
transform human relationships (6.14–15), change our attitude to money and possessions (6.19–24), and deliver us from
fear and anxiety (6.25–34). In all these realms legal rules and
regulations give way to openness to the Father who sets the
standards, penetrates the secret motives and provides the
resources. Everything comes to the light so completely in
relationship to him that his glory has to become the great goal
of our conduct. As the Kittel article puts it, "Faith in the
Father is an incentive to the sanctification of life"[10].

It is an incentive that both evangelical and charismatic
Christians need in our day if they are to grow. Jesus told us in
Acts 1.4 that the Spirit whom he was sending was "the promise of the Father", the one who came from the Father to relate
us to the Father, who came from the one who was complete
(*teleios*) to make us complete in him. As with Jesus we
cry in the Spirit Abba, Father, we shall become aware of
our sonship, ready for our inheritance, and open to our completeness.

1 In what follows I am dependent upon the article *Pater* by D. G. Schrenk
   and G. Quell in Volume 5 of the German original of Kittel's *Theological
   Dictionary of the New Testament*.
2 Helmut Thielicke *The Waiting Father* (James Clarke 1960) p27.

3 H. H. Farmer *The World and God* (Nisbet 1935) p25.
4 Joachim Jeremias *New Testament Theology* (Volume 1) (S.C.M. 1971) pp36–37 (cf the full discussion in J. D. G. Dunn: *Jesus and the Spirit* pp22–24 in which he maintains that Jeremias' conclusions, though in need of qualification, are essentially correct.)
5 ibid. p65.
6 ibid. p63.
7 ibid. p67.
8 C. F. D. Moule *The Holy Spirit* (Mowbrays 1978) p29.
9 C . B. Cranfield *The Epistle to the Romans* (International Critical Commentary; T. & T. Clark 1975) ad loc.
10 G. Kittel *Theologisches Woerterbuch zum N.T.* (Volume 5) p992 (W. Kohlhammer Verlag Stuttgart).

Chapter Three

Father and Son

We have seen that the Christian's cry to Abba has both a historical location and a charismatic eventfulness, but it has also a doctrinal content. To cry Abba may be a transforming spiritual experience, but it is authenticated as distinctively Christian only when it is related to the witness of scripture and set within the whole context of God's revelation and action in Christ. Thus we have to ask some theological questions, the answers to which cannot simply be read off from our own inner experience.

What exactly was Jesus saying about his relationship to God when he called him Father? What is the importance of that relationship for the whole structure of the gospel? In what sense is the relationship between Jesus and his Father unique and to what extent can others share in it? Since our relationship to Abba is clearly secondary to Jesus' own relationship, as a reflection is to an original, we need to examine his before we can know about ours.

To raise such questions is inevitably to become involved in the Christological debate about the person and status of Jesus which is rightly the chief concern of British theology at the present time. Is the traditional answer that Jesus Christ is the eternal Son of God incarnate and made man, still necessary or indeed possible; can we, or indeed must we learn to speak of him in other categories which will preserve all that matters of the New Testament witness, but will be intelligible and significant to modern man in the world of the twentieth century? Such a discussion is obviously concerned with questions of the first order of Christian importance and, without becoming too technically involved in the debate, we shall have to face them if we are going to say anything that is relevant about the relationship of Father and Son.

Our task is really to unpack the meaning, for the New Testament gospel and for ourselves, of Paul's terse trinitarian phrase in Galatians 4.6 where he speaks of God "sending the Spirit of his Son . . . crying 'Abba! Father!' ". What part does this Father/Son relationship between Jesus and God play in the structure and theology of the New Testament gospel? The Abba utterances may only be three in number, but when we widen our gaze to the Greek *Pater*, we see that the word is nothing less than a quintessential concentration of the central conviction out of which Jesus lived and worked. If we do not know that Jesus related to God as his Father, we know nothing about him at all.

To this even the numerical statistics bear their own witness. In the whole Old Testament God is called Father fifteen times, in the New Testament 245 times; three times in Mark, four times in the Q source, thirty-one times elsewhere in Matthew, four times in the Lucan source, and no less than a hundred times in John. It may well be true *historically* that John puts more Father-sayings on the lips of Jesus than the rest of the gospel tradition warranted, but it is equally true *theologically* that the idea which he highlighted in this way – the relation between God and Jesus – was the central one for the truth of the whole Christian claim. Jesus was who he was, and was both accepted and rejected as such "because he called God his own Father making himself equal with God" (John 5.18)

That John had a good historical basis for this theological concentration upon the unique relationship of Jesus to the Father is demonstrated by the passage in Matthew 11.25–30 (parallelled in Luke 10.22), usually attributed to the Q source, in which Father and Son and their relationship to each other are spoken of in a way that is markedly reminiscent of John, so that the passage, in the words of Karl von Hase, "gives the impression of a thunderbolt fallen from the Johannine sky"[1] into the middle of synoptic pastures. Jesus' designation of himself as *ho Huios* the Son without further qualification, and the unique mutual knowledge of Father and Son accessible to no-one else except by their revelation is characteristic of John's Christology and appears elsewhere only in isolated suggestions.

Jeremias rejects any suggestion that this passage is a later intrusion into the gospel from the world of Hellenistic mysticism since, apart from other considerations, "language, style and structure . . . clearly assign the sayings to a semitic-speaking milieu"[2]. He finds it equally incredible and unconvincing that a Johannine saying should in fact have found its way into Matthew, since, to cite only one point, the words used here for knowledge and revelation (*epiginoskein* and *apokaluptein*) are not characteristic of John's vocabulary. Jeremias argues that all the probabilities point to the dependence being rather of John upon Matthew and concludes that "we may have here one of the *logia* of Jesus from which Johannine theology grew. Indeed without such points of departure in the synoptic tradition it would be a complete puzzle how Johannine theology could have originated at all. If then there is nothing against the authenticity of Matthew 11.27, the intrinsic connection that it has with the way in which Jesus addressed God as Abba is decisively in its favour"[3].

It is good to know that technical scholarship can make a better case for the authenticity of this passage than has sometimes been allowed, but of course if we happen on theological grounds to accept the Johannine Christology as the only estimate that is adequate to the person and work of Jesus, we shall not find it hard to accept that at the moment of high exaltation described in Matthew 11 he gave expression in the presence of his disciples to this unique relationship with the Father in which he knew himself to stand.

Having claimed the right to make positive use of this passage let us now look more closely at its content and note the following points that clearly emerge and which give us something of an outline programme for the chapters immediately ahead.

1 The context once again is praise and prayer, "I praise you Father, Lord of heaven and earth", and this becomes even more explicit in the Lucan parallel where the language is almost formally trinitarian, "At that time Jesus, full of joy through the Holy Spirit (*egalliasato en to pneumati to hagio*) said, 'I praise you Father'" (Luke 10.21). The relationship of Jesus to his Father cannot be contemplated from a position of academic detachment as the "wise and prudent" seek. It can be realised only as it is opened up by the Holy Spirit; the theology of it can be grasped only by communion with it, and the babes (*nepioi*) are qualified for that knowledge because they are not too sophisticated to praise. To be filled with the Spirit is indeed just to give praise and thanks to the Father (Ephesians 5.19–20). A theology that is not first a doxology will be excluded from the secret which in the Spirit the Father shares with the Son. *Pectus facit theologum* – it is the heart that makes the theologian!

2 Jeremias raises here a question about the content and time of the revelation that the Father has entrusted to the Son. What was revealed and when? He makes an interesting suggestion. "We are not told when and where Jesus received this revelation in which God disclosed himself to him like a father to his son. The aorist *paredothe* does, however, give us a hint. It suggests one particular occurrence. It is striking because (as in e.g. John 15.19–20) we would expect the present. Perhaps therefore we should take *paredothe* to refer to Jesus' baptism. Matthew 11.27 gives only a hint at the content of the revelation which was granted to Jesus. It lies in the words 'my Father'"[4]. The suggestion linking the revelation of Matthew 11 with the voice that spoke in Jesus' baptism (3.17) assuring him of his own status as Son in the context of his calling and anointing to his mission, is a significant one which we shall later explore.

3 This passage emphasises the dependence of the Son upon the Father. The Son is not the primary source or possessor of what he reveals to his disciples. It has first to be "handed over" (*paredothe* = traditioned) to him by his Father. Within the

relationship of Father and Son, there is a first and a second, and the second has to receive from the first. Furthermore, knowledge of the Son is the prerogative of the Father, so that to be himself known, the Son depends upon the revealing activity of the Father, "No-one knows the Son except the Father" (v.27). These are leading themes of Johannine Christology; what the Son says and does has to be received from the Father; no-one can know the Son or come to him unless the Father draws him.

4 As well as the obvious dependence of the Son upon the Father, the second upon the first, there is a complementary dependence the other way round, of the Father upon the Son, of the first upon the second. The Father has committed all things (*panta*) to the Son. He does not speak, act or give himself to be known apart from his Son. The Father has not lost the initiating control in revelation, because at every point the Son looks to him; he exercises his sovereignty, however, in essential communion with the Son, who is the agent and medium of the enactment and revelation of his will among men. "No-one knows the Father except the Son and those to whom the Son chooses to reveal him" (v.27).

5 From the last two points taken together, we can advance to a third. The relationship of Father and Son is unique and itself constitutive of the gospel. The very metaphor of Father and Son implies not only mutual dependence, but shared life and being. That is why in the biblical tradition it is used with such reserve of the relationship between Creator and creature, but it is of the highest significance that the reserve is withdrawn just here, where *the* Father and *the* Son are spoken of in such absolute terms as the sharers of a mutual knowledge of each other, which is exclusive to them and which is opened to others only by the will and choice of the partners to it. The implication that they know each other in a unique way be- cause they are one in a unique way lies very close at hand.

   In addition our passage makes clear that the relationship of Father and Son is not only the way in which the knowledge of God reaches us, but is itself an essential and constituent part of what we know. To know God is to know the Father through the Son and the Son through the Father. Jesus is not just the prophet of God who speaks of and points to a truth of which he is the adventitious and inessential mouthpiece, so that it could be as well revealed through some other spokesman, without itself being altered. Jesus, however, is not in that sense the mere minister of God's truth, he is an essential part of its content. To know God is to know this relationship between Father in heaven and Son on earth.

This is nowhere clearer in this passage than when Jesus turns from addressing himself to his Father and calls to the weary and heavy laden around him. "Come to *me* and *I* will give you rest. Take my yoke upon you and learn from me." The invitation implies the same high Christology as the prayer. Many can say, Go to God, but only Jesus can say Come to me, for to come to him *is* to come to God. The Father is *Kurios*, Lord of heaven and earth, and Jesus is meek and lowly, yet from the midst of that humility and humanity there ring out the accents of the divine authority that he shares with the Father.

God's revelation and God's saving action are effected within this mutual relationship of Father and Son, ultimately because that relationship is constitutive of the very life of God himself. We stand here in this passage at the beginning of a doctrinal development which leads straight to the Christology of St John, and which ultimately it took the doctrine of the Trinity to define and defend. The essential togetherness of Father and Son which is the central thread of that development is clearly present here at its very beginning. In gospel truth and in Christian practice Father and Son belong together. A Father who is not the Father of Jesus will not long continue to be a Father to us; a Jesus who is not Son of God will not long continue to be Saviour of men.

We have used the Matthew 11 passage to make in a preliminary way some of the main points we must take up in detail, centred upon the mutual dependence of Father and Son. In this chapter we shall discuss that dependence from one side, the dependence of the Father upon the Son, and in the next chapter from the other, the dependence of the Son upon the Father.

The Dependence of the Father upon the Son
We have seen from Matthew 11 – at this point a summary of much else in the gospels – that it is both God's nature and will that as Father he should speak and act through his Son, Jesus. What this means we may discuss in several points.

1 The Father has his *identity* through and in his Son. So John 1.18, "No man has seen God at any time, but the only begotten God (*monogenes theos*, or alternatively the only begotten Son, *monogenes huios*) who is at the Father's side, has made him known." The strong reading "only begotten God" has support from some of the chief uncial manuscripts and is preferred by the Bible Society Greek text.

This text makes two points about the identity of Jesus and the Father. (i) The Father has his identity in the Son because it is the Son who has made him known. But (ii) the Father is in fact identical with the Son in being and nature. The Father is God the unbegotten, but the Son also is *monogenes theos* – God the only begotten. Karl Barth makes it a basic principle of his theology that the first is only possible because of the second, that only God can reveal God, that in order to be an adequate revelation of the Father, Jesus has to share the nature and being of the Father.

Let us, however, for the moment confine ourselves to the first and simpler point that the nature and character of God's fatherhood is in the New Testament defined by Jesus. This is common ground for all the New Testament writers who touch the matter. Peter and Paul alike define him in that way – he is the God and Father of our Lord Jesus Christ (e.g. in II Corinthians 1.3, Ephesians 1.3, I Peter 1.3). The nature both of his Godhead and of his fatherhood can be discovered only by approaching him in relationship to Jesus Christ. This, says the Kittel article, is "an expressive description of the distinctive content of the New Testament understanding of God"[5].

Before we examine the positive meaning of the definition of

God's fatherhood by Christ, we should first explore the important negative implications it involves. If God's fatherhood is identified and defined by Christ, it follows that it is not to be identified and defined by anything else.

a God's fatherhood is not to be defined as his universal and natural relationship as Creator to all men. The New Testament knows as well as the Old that God is the Creator of all men, but, like the Old, that is not what it means when it speaks of his fatherhood. He is not firstly and primarily the Father of all men, but rather the Father of the Lord Jesus Christ, and his fatherhood means the intimate bond of love and authority, and ultimately of nature and being, that unites him to his Son, and that only through that Son becomes relevant to all other men. To be a child of God in the New Testament does not mean to be human, so that all men would as such be God's children. To be a child of God in an experiential sense is to be in that relationship of trust in God's love and obedience to God's authority and participation in God's life and fellowship of which Jesus is the origin and possibility. God's fatherhood becomes universal not in relation to his creative act in the past, but in virtue of his eschatological act in the future and universal glory will be given to the Father when every tongue confesses and every knee bows to the Son (Philippians 2.10–11). Creator and Father are not to be separated, but neither are they to be confused; the fatherhood of the Creator is in the first place his fatherhood of Jesus Christ.

b God's fatherhood is not to be defined by *projection* either. It is not human fatherhood thrown on to the screen of the heavens and given infinite dimensions.

There is obviously a very close psychological connection between our experiences of human fatherhood and our approach to God's fatherhood. The whole notion of fatherhood in whatever context it arises is highly emotive. It is surrounded by conscious memories, half-hidden loves, longings and resentments; you have only to speak for a few minutes to a group of ordinary people about God the Father to see that they are deeply involved in reactions that are at a far deeper level than the merely intellectual, and which say something about the homes in which they grew up and the presence or absence, in many different senses of those words, of their own fathers. Unless the whole image of fatherhood is corrected or even redeemed, we shall almost inevitably project onto God the father we have loved or missed, have desired or resented, so that our adult spiritual life will be secretly controlled by our reactions to our early family life.

When that happens the God we worship may be made in the image of a tyrant to whom we have to submit, or against whom we have to rebel; he may be needed and required to give us the compensating care and love that our human fathers did not or could not give. Because of their failure we may have endless and only dimly comprehended doubts about our heavenly Father's care and accessibility, or our spiritual life may be clouded by our endlessly continued teenage rebellion against the wrong, or even the right kind of parental authority. We may be weighed down by great guilt and anxiety that we cannot be acceptable to our heavenly Father because we were never sure if we were acceptable to our earthly father, especially if he tended to judge us by our achievements. Natural religion is at this point natural attitudes to our fathers projected on to the heavens in some of these ways.

But the heavens are not empty, nor are they a blank screen to reflect back our fantasies. "No-one has ever gone into heaven except the one who came from heaven – the Son of Man" (John 3.13). The authentic projector points not from earth to heaven to screen our images on a divine scale; rather it points from heaven to earth to screen God's own image on a human scale. The one valid projection and image of the Father is his own Son come from him to be made man among us. He comes to show us the one who is my Father before he is your Father (John 20.17). The Christian norm of fatherhood and sonship is the dealings between God and Jesus; the love with which Jesus was loved and to which he trusted is the Father's love and not any other, the authority that he exercised is the Father's authority and not any other.

In the incarnation Jesus defines the fatherhood of God in relation to the image of human fatherhood that he found in Israel and which we outlined in the last chapter. In so far as that image is God-given he confirms it, in so far as it has been distorted by human limitations and sinfulness, he corrects and renews it. This he does not mainly in a theoretical way by teaching and articulating a new ideal of fatherhood, but much more by the trust and obedience with which he lives among his disciples and dies on the cross.

Just as he begins to redefine fatherhood over against the ideas of that ancient paternalistic society, so still the fatherhood revealed in the life and death of Jesus confirms and resists, transforms and redeems all the images, conscious and unconscious, of experienced human fatherhood that we bring to it in our very different society. If the severe and authoritarian ancient image of paternity in Israel needed to be corrected in terms of the love and compassion of the one who received the prodigal; so the modern image, indulgent, nonprescriptive, often detached and unsupportive needs to be corrected in a different direction.

When my own son was at primary school he brought home a picture he had drawn, the central figure in which was a man in black, with a newspaper held out at arm's length in front of him, veiling him from everything else and completely absorbing his attention. "Who is that supposed to be?" I asked. "Why, you of course." Fathers in the ministry have especially to beware at this point. Our calling connects us closely with God in our children's eyes, and we sometimes have sons and daughters who deeply resent the heavenly Father, because we have portrayed him as the one who has called us away to endless meetings and pastoral commitments, to love and look after everybody else but them. We have all not just doctrines to teach, but sins to confess at this point – and I as much as any.

But the Saviour comes – the one who saves the image of fatherhood from what we have made of it as much as anything else, and in so doing turns the hearts of the fathers to their children.

The image of fatherhood that God gives in Jesus is a powerful one, but it does not undo the damage of false fatherhood by entering into cerebral competition with it. People are not changed by reading books on the New Testament doctrine of God's fatherhood. The new image that comes from Jesus has to penetrate to the deep subconscious springs of life and memory where the old images and reactions have their seat. It is the work of the Holy Spirit to cry Abba, Father at precisely these deep places of our hearts and spirits, there to begin to transform us and set us free, and bit by bit bring us out of the neglect or tyranny of the fatherhood we remember, into the sure love and liberating obedience of the God and Father of Jesus. At this point the great healer of the memories is the Spirit of the Son who spells out Father for us again and again till we are free of the old and believe the new.

The point we have been making is made in the New Testament in Ephesians 3.15 to which we shall be returning. Suffice to say now that there it is quite clear that the norm of fatherhood is not in us but in God "from whom all fatherhood in earth and heaven takes its name". Karl Barth makes the theological point quite clearly, "It is . . . not that there is first of all human fatherhood and then a so-called divine fatherhood, but just the reverse; true and proper fatherhood resides in God and from this fatherhood what we know as fatherhood among us men is derived"[6]. That is not only good theology; it is also liberation to many captives of neglect, guilt and fear.

c There is nothing *sexist* about the New Testament doctrine of the fatherhood of God. This is a point that has hardly needed to be made before in Christian history but certainly needs to be made today. God is the God and Father of our Lord Jesus Christ; the very formula makes it clear that here the relationship and contrast is Father/Son and not Father/Mother. It is true that it was defined in the context of a patriarchal rather than a matriarchal society, but this is a point at which the gospel transcended the situation in which it found expression. There is in the doctrine of God's fatherhood no pagan attempt to assert masculinity at the expense of femininity. The love of

God the Father revealed in Jesus Christ is the original, although not the projection of all our human loves, and fulfils and holds them all together inside itself, the authority of father, but the tender care and encouragement of mother also. The *patria* which in Ephesians 3.15 takes its name from God includes mother love as much as father love in itself. In Jesus Christ there is all strength and all tenderness, and the one who has seen him has seen the Father.

Within the Old Testament God in his loving is compared to a mother as well as to a father, "Can a mother forget the baby at her breast and have no compassion on the child she has borne? Though she may forget, yet I will not forget you" (Isaiah 49.15). The love that the human mother displays failingly and imperfectly, the heavenly Father shows perfectly and completely. In Christ there is that same tenderness "I am meek and lowly in heart and you shall find rest for your souls" (Matthew 11.29) and the Holy Spirit, the Paraclete, knows how to pour tender consolation as well as bracing encouragement into our hearts.

One of the few sayings of the short-lived Pope John Paul I reported in the press was his remark that "God is not only our Father but also our Mother". It is said to have shocked some ultra-orthodox cardinals. They should have listened, because it is precisely when the love of God is denied its motherly quality and is developed in a masculine, authoritarian and therefore sexist direction, that compensating images of the tender gentle Jesus or of the Virgin Mother have to be evolved, to whom people can run from the stern judgements and harsh demands of God. But it is not the ministry of the Lord Jesus Christ or of Mary his mother to compensate for what is lacking in the love of the Father; it is rather their function, in their quite different ways, for Christ to be the archetypal revelation of it, and for Mary to be in her special way one of its first and most excellent reflections.

Thus, to summarise some of the ways in which God's fatherhood is not to be defined, we may say not *naturally* as a universal relationship between Creator and created, not *analogically* by the projection of earthly originals, not *sexually* to affirm a masculine as against a feminine love – but always, and here is the positive, Christologically "The only Son, who is in the bosom of the Father, he has made him known" (John 1.18).

We are now to explore that positive and ask what it means that the Father is dependent upon the Son for his identity.

2 The words and works of Jesus Christ are the normative expression not only of his own person and nature, but also of the action, person and nature of the Father. The basic conviction and claim of Jesus is that his word is the word of God, and that his action is the action of God – because ultimately his being is identical with the being of God. Leaving aside the identity of being for later, we concentrate at the moment on the Identity of action between the Father and the Son. "The Father is working still, and I am working" (John 5.17). The union between Father and Son is in the first place dynamic, eventful, directed towards the achievement of an end, and the action of the Father is defined and expressed in the action of the Son. "Don't you believe that I am in the Father, and that the Father is in me?" Jesus asks his disciples in John 14.10 and the context makes it clear that the primary reference here is not to a mystical or metaphysical unity but to an identity in agency and action. "The words I say to you are not just my own. Rather, it is the Father, living in me, who is doing his work. Believe me when I say that I am in the Father and the Father is in me; or at least believe me on the evidence of the miracles themselves" (John 14.10–11). Notice here that the words of Jesus are identified with the work of God. The word he speaks is not merely something that possesses a truth content, it is something that has power to effect what is spoken, to work the work of God and to further his purpose.

God's truth always stands in the closest connection with God's action, his revelation with his salvation. The demonstration of the union between Father and Son is the mighty works of Jesus in which his agency and that of the Father are each in its different way involved. The God of the New Testament is not some inert and passive ground of all being,

into whose eternal and unchanging nature Jesus opens a
window and lets us look. On the contrary he is the God who
changes things, whose speaking and doing leave nothing as he
found it. He makes himself known as the one who acts, who
makes the lame walk and the blind see and the dead rise. He is
the Father who works salvation and whose working is known
and effective through the agency of his Son. There is no work
of the Son which is not also a work of the Father. That has to
do with the dependence of Jesus upon God and will be ex-
amined in the next chapter. But the converse is also true, that
there is for the New Testament no work of the Father which is
not also a work of the Son.

The extraordinary Christian claim is that the coming, living,
dying and rising of Jesus of Nazareth is the indispensable clue
to God's purpose in creation, his universal will of redemption,
and to final judgement at the end. The indispensable and
essential partner of God in making all things, reconciling all
things, judging all things is the one who became man as Jesus
and as such is also Messiah and Lord. That has been a scandal
from the beginning, and the attack against it that is at the
heart of much contemporary academic theology of a radical
persuasion shows that it is scandal still.

Nevertheless, that Jesus is the essential partner of the
Father in all his works and ways with men and with the world is
one of the basic assumptions of all the New Testament writers, which again and again comes to explicit expression in
what they say about creation, redemption, the last things.

a The Father works through the Son in regard to creation. So
John 1.3, "Through him (*di'autou*) all things were made;
apart from him (*choris autou*) nothing was made that has been
made." In the same vein (Colossians 1.15-17), "He is the
image of the invisible God, the firstborn over all creation. For
by him (*en auto*) all things were created in heaven and on
earth . . . all things were created by him (*di'autou*) and for
him (*eis auton*). He is before all things and in him all things
hold together." Jesus Christ is the agent, principle of cohesion
and final purpose of all creation so that it is impossible to

speak about God's work in creation out of relation to him. So also in Hebrews 1.2 the Son through whom God has now spoken to us is he "through whom (*di'autou*) he made the universe." Dr James Houston draws attention to the quite remarkable fact that such New Testament evidence establishes, namely, that "within a few years of the death and resurrection of Jesus, it was widely recognised in these Christian communities that Christ is Co-Creator"[7]. Thus the New Testament provides us with the basis of a theology of nature, that, just as much as the theology of salvation, takes its starting point from God's action in Christ, but no basis at all for a natural theology that wants to think about nature from some other starting point than Jesus Christ, and so approaches nature without knowledge of its central purpose and significance. What all this means we shall spell out a little in a later chapter. Sufficient for now our main point; in creation the Father does not act without the Son.

b In salvation the Father does not act without the Son. Restored right relationship with God is uniquely and essentially dependent upon the life, death and resurrection of Jesus, which is God's only and yet universal provision of reconciliation and salvation which is to be made known to all men. To say that in its own distinctive way is the *raison d'être* of every important New Testament affirmation of the gospel.

In this John and Paul speak for all the rest, "God so loved the world that he gave his only Son, that whoever believes in him should not perish but have eternal life" (John 3.16). Jesus is the expression of God's saving love and the object of man's saving faith. "All this is from God, who reconciled us to himself through Christ and gave us the ministry of reconciliation: that God was reconciling the world to himself in Christ, not counting men's sins against them. And he has committed to us the message of reconciliation" (II Corinthians 5.18–19). God's action moves from the one to the many, from a single centre in Christ to a universal destination in all the world.

In his book *On Being a Christian*, the Roman Catholic theologian Hans Küng challenges this unique connection be-

tween God's act of salvation and Jesus Christ, as quite inadequate to the modern awareness of the rich religious plurality
of the world in which Christianity is but one way of salvation
among many. Like many before him Küng finds the Christian
insistence upon the unique status of Jesus as God's unique
agent of salvation intolerably intolerant and narrowminded.
He assumes without argument that each religion has its own
access to God's salvation, but, in his desire as Christian theologian to do justice to Jesus Christ, he says that he is the one
definitive revelation of God's truth. He writes, "The question
of truth and the question of salvation are not to be confused,
as they were formerly in Christian theology. The modern
Christian 'theology of religions' is right in saying that people
can attain salvation in other religions and in this sense the
latter can reasonably be called 'ways of salvation'. But the
question of salvation does not make the question of truth
superfluous. If Christian theology today asserts that all men –
even in the world religions – can be saved, this certainly does
not mean that all religions are equally true . . . They do not
offer *the* truth for Christians"[8].

This statement owes whatever degree of plausibility it may
be judged to possess to the vagueness and generality of the
main terms it uses. What is this salvation which is universally
available apart from knowledge of God's truth? How is it to
be defined and how obtained? To that there are as many
answers as there are religions, and unless we have some norm
to define what salvation means, the whole matter gets lost in a
woolly cloud of relativity where we hardly know what we are
talking about. If one replies that the truth about salvation is,
according to Küng, the truth as it is in Christ, then one is left
with the paradox that people can be said to be saved, who
either do not know about or else explicitly reject what Christ
means by salvation, and who pursue salvation under presuppositions and by methods that both sides agree are in blatant
contradiction with the truth in Christ. Their salvation is not
seen as being *from* sin, *by* grace, *through* faith in Jesus, *into*
new fellowship with the Father *in* the Spirit – but in altogether different terms. Yet the truth in Christ which other

notions of salvation contradict in these ways, is somehow the truth about these other salvations also.

And even if we can see our way through such a strange situation, we still have to ask ourselves if in New Testament terms one can have a Christ who is still *the* truth (in a unique and special sense so that Küng still italicises the definite article), but who is not *the* way or *the* life, but only one of many possible different ways to life with God. In New Testament terms a salvation which does not as an integral part of itself bring us to the knowledge of the truth is inconceivable, because truth and salvation are basically alternative descriptions of right relationship with the living God and fellowship with him, and both are inseparable from the action of God in Jesus Christ. "I am the way and the truth and the life. No-one comes to the Father except through me" (John 14.6). "Salvation is found in no-one else, for there is no other name under heaven given to men by which we must be saved" (Acts 4.12).

Such statements are not based on experiential encounters with the richness of world religions, far less are they negative reactions towards these religions; they are simply distinctive insights into the nature of what God has done in Christ. Salvation and access to the Father are so inextricably linked with the person and work of Jesus Christ that you cannot have them without him or him without them. What one then says in the light of that insight about world religions, and indeed about one's own culture and Christian tradition, is a matter of sensitive discernment and greater humility about their own continuing need of Christ's grace, than Christians have often shown. The fact that in the past Christian missions have absolutised the relative does not now mean that they should relativise the absolute, and if there is one absolute for Christians it is that our salvation is uniquely in the name of Christ. When that is abandoned it is doubtful if we can even give the men of other religions an account of ourselves, that is in any credible continuity with our New Testament origins.

We shall have a great deal more to say about the relation of Father and Son in the work of salvation in succeeding chapters. Enough to establish now our conviction that it is a unique and indissoluble one. The grace of God is universal in extent and intent, its only limitation is that it will be always and everywhere what it was at the beginning, the grace of the Lord Jesus Christ, that has its origin, content and meaning in him alone.

c The Father acts at the final consummation in relationship to Christ. One of the things that we *can* understand in the terrifying scenario of the book of Revelation is that it has at its centre the one who sits upon the throne and the Lamb, and it is in the mutuality of Father and Son, of Ancient of Days and Lamb, that the final consummation in its negative side as judgement and its positive as restoration, takes place. The Son is the executant of the Father's judgement and relationship to him is the norm of that judgement. To believe in him now is to anticipate that judgement, because in Christ the Judge has already come. "Whoever believes in him is not condemned, but whoever does not believe stands condemned already, because he has not believed in the name of God's one and only Son" (John 3.18).

Even in Paul's speech at Athens where his attitude to other religions is more open and liberal than anywhere else in the New Testament, he ends with an uncompromising assertion of the universal judgement of all men on the basis of their relationship to Jesus, "He has set a day when he will judge the world with justice by the man he has appointed. He has given proof of this to all men by raising him from the dead" (Acts 17.31). So also in John 5.22 where the distinctive activities of Father and Son in relation to judgement are made clear, "The Father judges no-one but has entrusted all judgement to the Son." The source of judgement is the Father, but the execution of it belongs to the Son. There is no way round Jesus when we are speaking of the judgement of God.

And if we are speaking about the positive side of the last things, the completion of the kingdom and the appearance of the new heaven and earth, the Christocentric concentration is every bit as unanimous. In Ephesians 1.10, when the times have reached their fulness, God's purpose is "to bring all things in heaven and on earth together under one head, even Christ", and in Philippians 2 it is his name that is above every name, which every tongue is to confess and at which every knee is to bow (2.9–11), even though in this consummation the priority of the Father is still marked and real (cf I Corinthians 15.28).

Thus all the way from creation at the beginning, through the incarnation at the centre, to final redemption at the end, God speaks and acts through Jesus Christ. The love of God is not any ideal of love, it is that love that in the specific grace of Jesus Christ comes to seek and to save what was lost, to establish at great cost fellowship with those who never had and could not ever have any kind of claim upon it. The power of God is not any kind of sovereign omnipotence, it is that specific power by which the Son became man, and which he used with compassion to heal the sick and endure the cross; it is the power by which he rose from the dead. The truth of God is not the content of any philosophical world-vision, or mystic communication or charismatic insight; the truth of God is the person and action of his Son who is both Messiah of Israel and Lord of the Church, to whose coming prophets bore witness before, and apostles after, and that witness is interpreted out of scripture by the Spirit in the Church. The commandment of God is not any ethical action or religious discipline, it is the commandment of the Father that is defined in this gospel by this Son. The Father has committed all things to the Son and nobody knows the Father except the Son and those to whom he chooses to reveal him.

1 Karl von Hase *Die Geschichte Jesus* (Leipzig 1876) p 422.
2 J. Jeremias *New Testament Theology* (Vol. 1) (S.C.M. 1975) p 57.
3 ibid. p 59.
4 ibid. p 6.
5 Quell and Schrenk: Art. on *Pater* in Kittel. *Theologisches Woerterbuch* Vol. 5, p 1109.
6 Karl Barth *Dogmatics in Outline* (S.C.M. 1949) p 43.
7 James Houston *I Believe in the Creator* (Hodder & Stoughton 1979) p 159.
8 Hans Küng *On Being a Christian* (E. T. Collins 1976) p 104.

Chapter Four

Son and Father

In the last chapter we spoke of the dependence of the Father upon the Son for his identity, revelation and action. This is the very real dependence of the senior upon the junior, of the first upon the second, of the initiator upon the executant – which is familiar enough in many spheres of life and holds good here also.

Now we look at the same relationship the other way round and see the dependence of the Son upon the Father. If it is true that Jesus defines God, it is just as true that God defines Jesus; if only the Son knows the Father, equally only the Father knows the Son. Looking at the relationship from this side makes us feel much more at home, because we also depend on the Father. The Son relates to his Father as one of us, as man in the midst of our humanity and his sonship in all its uniqueness and distinctness is relevant to and exemplary and enabling for us. As the *monogenes theos* (John 1.18) he is unique and incomparable but in his incarnation he has become "the eldest in a large family of brothers" (Romans 8.29 NEB) so that we might in our way share his sonship. In the words of John 1.12, "To all who received him, to those who believed in his name, he gave the right to become children of God (*tekna theou*)." The similarity and dissimilarity between his sonship and ours is the special concern of Chapter Seven, but as now we look at his dependence on his Father, there will be many points at which we are reminded of our own.

1 Jesus receives his identity from the Father. This is the converse of the point from which we started the last chapter. Jesus needed, not just once, but again and again for each stage of his mission and each crisis in his living and dying, a freshly confirmed knowledge of his own identity. Each time he came to know who he was by coming to know again who God was – through a fresh confession of Abba in the power of the Holy Spirit.

Some of the existential reality and agony of that question of identity is memorably expressed in one of Dietrich Bonhoeffer's poems entitled simply *Who am I?* Bonhoeffer recalls how others in prison with him say they have found him brave, calm and cheerful and compares that with what he has felt like inside.

> Am I then really all that which other men tell of?
> Or am I only what I know of myself,
> Restless and longing and sick like a bird in a cage
> Struggling for breath as though hands were compressing
>   my throat,
> Yearning for colours, for flowers, for the voices of birds,
> Thirsting for words of kindness, for neighbourliness
> Trembling with anger at despotisms and petty
>   humiliation,
> Tossing in expectation of great events,
> Powerlessly trembling for friends at an infinite distance,
> Weary, and empty at praying, at thinking, at
>   making,
> Faint and ready to say farewell to it all?
> Who am I? This or the other?
> Am I one person today and another tomorrow?
> Am I both at once? A hypocrite before others,
> And before myself a contemptibly woebegone weakling?
> Or is something within me still like a beaten army,
> Fleeing in disorder from victory already achieved?
> Who am I? They mock me, these lonely questions of
>   mine.
> Whoever I am, though knowest, O God, I am thine.[1]

Can we not hear in that a faint echo of Gethsemane? At any rate it reminds us that the question of identity is a human and agonising one, and that the answer to it for both the Man and his men is not in themselves but in God. We live in a world facing identity crises at many levels where individuals and communities are looking sometimes wildly in all sorts of directions to discover who they are.

Some look to introspection, and seek their identity on a psychiatrist's couch. The result is sometimes more disintegration than identification: we peel all the layers from the onion, and find that at the centre there is nothing at all. Others look less inward than backward: the popularity of the novel *Roots*[2], the use made of the Mormon genealogical research services, the resistance to the contemporary lapse into featureless anonymity that modern nationalism represents, are symptoms of our need to define ourselves in terms of the past from which we have sprung.

Still others look outward to their achievements for definition. We often say of someone that he wants to make something of himself, hoping by successful activity to establish his identity. *Ago ergo sum*, I do, therefore I am, would perhaps be the modern activist equivalent of Descartes' dictum.

In effect Jesus related to all these ways of identifying himself. He knew his Father in deep inward experience, and yet did not trust to the experience itself but only to the reality and the authority of the one who spoke in it. His roots were of the best and deepest, the Son of David in the royal line of Israel's greatest promise. But he was free and creative in regard to that tradition; he shaped it more than it shaped him, because his ultimate dependence was not upon it, but upon his heavenly Father. Nobody came behind him in achievements. He had a long catalogue of happenings behind him to prove his claim to a Baptist (Matthew 11.4–6) who began to doubt his messianic identity. But the achievements are the fruit rather than the source of his confidence as to who he is. Adoptionist Christologies teach that Jesus became the Son of God because of the life he lived and the works he did, but the New Testament is different – his works flow from his sonship.

Because he is a Son, he heals and seeks and saves; his ministry is his obedience to his identity rather than his way of achieving it. His relationship to God comes before his action for him.

Thus through experience, within the context of tradition, as the determining factor of the mission that is to follow, Jesus is given his identity by his Father. As Sir Norman Anderson has put it, his knowledge of his sonship "did not principally lie in a subjective consciousness of his own identity, but in an intimate knowledge of God as his Father"[3]. He goes on to quote the French theologian Louis Bouyer to the effect that "Jesus was the 'Christ, the Son of the living God' not directly by knowing that he was, but because he knew God *as the Father* . . . What is unique in the consciousness of Jesus of Nazareth is that it was pierced and traversed, from its first awakening, by that intuition, which was to precede, penetrate and saturate all his states of consciousness"[4].

In other words Christ's knowledge of himself as Son was not intrinsic but was a reflex of his special knowledge of the Father. He knew himself as he knew God. We may with profit look at some of the gospel instances in which that becomes clear.

a He discovered his adulthood in discovering the Father. Much of the significance of the story in Luke 2 of Jesus staying behind in the temple when Mary and Joseph left Jerusalem for home lies in the fact that it happened in the year when he attained his Jewish adulthood as a *bar Mitzvah*. What moved his relationship to his parents into second place and made him to that extent independent of them was a new realisation that God was his Father, and as such had first and incomparable claim on his attention, loyalty and obedience; he must be about his Father's business. Here his very first recorded word in this gospel, like his very last from the cross (23.46) is about his relationship to his Father. This is Luke's way of saying that with Jesus his heavenly Father came first and last and at all points in between. And to know his Father from the very first brings him under a divine constraint of obedience, "I must (*dei*) be about my Father's business" (2.49). As Marshall puts it, there is here "a momentary glimpse through a curtain into a private room"[5] – into the holy of holies of this young life to whom there has come a unique insight that engenders what is to prove the overmastering compulsion of his whole life. Soon he will return to his boyhood obedience (2.51) but the maturing centre of his life has been discovered and revealed. The boy who belonged to Mary has begun to be the man who belongs to God.

b The realisation of God's fatherhood and his own sonship has a decisive part at the baptism of Jesus. As he emerges from the water and offers himself for the work to which he has been called, two things happen that are very intimately connected – the voice of God speaks and the Spirit of God descends. In almost exact parallel with the later Christian experience recorded in Romans 8.15 ff, a new awareness of sonship and a new release of the Spirit's activity are closely connected. As he becomes aware that he is Son, so he enters into the *kleronomia*, the inheritance of the Son, which, as we saw, is in the end death and resurrection. "If sons then heirs, if *the* Son, then *the* heir". In the new confidence of sonship he begins to exercise in a new way the authority of the Spirit which is his birthright.

In the word that is spoken to him, "You are my Son, whom I love; with you I am well pleased" (Luke 3.22), there are almost certainly echoes of three most significant Old Testament texts. (i) A *messianic* greeting echoing Psalm 2 where the reference is to the messianic king chosen and equipped by God for a universal task of restoration and rule, "You are my Son; today I have become your Father. Ask of me, and I will make the nations your inheritance, the ends of the earth your possession" (Psalm 2.7–8). (ii) There is a reference to the *servant* of Jahweh as he is described in Isaiah 42.1. "Here is my servant (*pais*) whom I uphold, my chosen one (*eklektos* in LXX) in whom I delight." Notice that in Luke *pais*, servant has become *huios* son, and *eklektos*, chosen, has become *agapetos*, beloved, which, when used with son or daughter, means "only" (See Marshall ad loc.). (iii) The third reference is to Genesis 22.2, 12, 16 where Isaac in the context of the commanded sacrifice on Mount Moriah is in the LXX referred to in precisely this language, *ho huios sou ho agapetos*, "your only and beloved son". This is a clear reference to *sacrifice*. What Abraham was at the last moment excused from giving, God himself is now making ready to give – his only and beloved Son.

In thus fulfilling the three Old Testament themes as Son who is also messiah, servant and sacrifice, Jesus will also fill them out and give them a content and a unity that they lacked before. At the very moment at which Jesus acknowledges afresh this new vision of his sonship, the Holy Spirit comes down upon him. By that Spirit he is anointed for the mission of a Son who will suffer sacrifice as servant, but come into his own as king.

One of the major themes of Luke's account of Jesus' temptation in the wilderness is the attack that is launched on this consciousness of sonship that has come to him in his baptism. The casting of doubt on his sonship is the starting point of the first and third temptations which begin, "If you are the Son of God" (Luke 4.3 and 9) and so challenge the authority and validity of the voice that spoke to him as he emerged from the Jordan. In the first temptation he is attacked at the point of his obedience – he is to use his power to meet his own need for bread rather than in obedience to his Father's word to him. To fall from sonship is to fall from a life that has God and his word at the centre, to a life that takes its bearings from human need and ultimately our own needs. Against it Jesus affirms that his life draws its strength and meaning from his obedience to his Father. "Man does not live on bread alone" (4.4).

In the third temptation the attack is on his trust in what his Father has said to him. It is a temptation to prove his sonship because basically he no longer believes it, and the experimental leap will provide just the proof he needs. He is to use charismatic power to demonstrate to others, but chiefly to himself, that he has the superior status of a Son. It is not enough that his Father has said it, he has to establish it by signs and wonders. But this temptation also is exposed and defeated. God is to be trusted, not tested, "Do not put the Lord your God to the test" (4.12).

The appropriate relationship of a son to a father is one of dependence, which consists of obedient trust and trustful obedience, and it is significant that the attack comes at precisely these two vital points. If Jesus fails here at the beginning, his whole mission will fail before it has started. These are in fact the two classic charismatic temptations, and the dubious side of the charismatic movement is made up of those who misuse spiritual power to satisfy their own needs for healing, peace, excitement or to establish their status as the possessors of gifts or performers of signs – all because they have not really believed or obeyed their sonship.

With the temptations over and his trust and obedience unsullied and reaffirmed, Jesus comes to Nazareth in the confidence and assurance that he is the obedient Son who has believed all that his Father has said to him and who therefore has the boldness and expectation that can come only from intimate and unbroken relationship with God. He is free from himself and free for his Father; he knows who his Father is and therefore who he himself is. He is the Son on whom the favour and the Spirit of the Father rest. Therefore he can go forward against all human opposition knowing that the Father is with him and will honour the word that he speaks and the hand that he stretches out to heal.

This confidence in the Father is the *sine qua non* of New Testament boldness (*parrhesia*). If we are in doubt about God's fatherly attitude towards us, we shall be shrinking, grovelling and unexpectant in our prayers; and we shall hold back, play safe and refuse to take risks in his service, in fear that at the crucial moment God will not back us up. Everyone who has ever prayed for anyone else's healing knows this. No matter how experienced we may be, each time we undertake this ministry all our doubts about God's willingness and our worthiness crowd in upon us, and we have to appeal back to the atoning work of Christ which establishes God's favour and our standing, and also to the Holy Spirit who by crying Abba in our hearts witnesses anew that he is Father and we are his loved and accepted children. As with Jesus, so with us, the power and gifts of the Holy Spirit can be received and used rightly in God's service only by those who know that they are his sons.

c At the hour of critical decision as he turns towards Calvary, Jesus has again to be told who he is. He has announced to his disciples that he is going to Jerusalem to suffer and die. The transfiguration is the confirmation of that choice, which comes first of all from the law and the prophets, through their typical representatives, Moses and Elijah – who speak to him about his exodus (Greek *exodos*) – which means both his death, and the redemptive departure from the house of bondage which it will accomplish. It is as Messiah of Israel and Servant of God, in fulfilment of God's revelation and promise to his ancient people that he goes to die.

But the greater confirmation comes, as at his baptism, directly from the voice of God himself, repeating the words first spoken at Jordan with two significant differences. (i) *Agapetos* (beloved = only) is replaced by *eklelegmenos* (chosen); the former emphasises his unique status as Son, the latter his unique mission as servant and saviour. (ii) *Autou Akouete* (hear him) replaces "with whom I am well pleased". As he goes the way of obedient suffering he has a new right to be heard, a new authority among men. As he glorifies the Father in his death so the Father prepares to glorify him with a new authentication of his mission. Sonship means being chosen for costly obedience, but also being brought into possession of that authority.

d In Gethsemane as he enters his agony Jesus finds his strength in again affirming his relationship to Abba. He is able to take the cup, which means God's wrath, rejection and judgement (Psalm 11.6; 75.8 Isaiah 51.17 etc.), because the hand that offers it is still the hand of his Father. There was involved in this transaction not simply prayer and pleading from Jesus, but revelation and strengthening from the Father, as Luke makes clear in his mention of the angel. Amidst his agony "an

angel from heaven appeared to him and strengthened him"
(22.43) and in the strength of that communion with his Father
he can face his passion.

e That is further emphasised by Luke in that two of the words
from the cross which he reports are Abba words. (i) "Father,
forgive them for they do not know what they are doing"
(23.34). The absence of that sentence from some important
manuscripts has thrown doubt upon it, although such a prayer
by Jesus is surely presupposed by Luke's account of the dying
prayer of Stephen in Acts 7.60. The point that it makes is clear
and central, that the forgiveness of others is mediated through
the prayer of Jesus to the Father made on the cross. (ii) "Jesus
called out with a loud voice. 'Father, into your hands I commit
my spirit.' When he had said this, he breathed his last"
(23.46). Luke does not follow Matthew and Mark in reporting
Jesus' cry of dereliction, the one prayer significantly not addressed to Abba, because it is prayed from the place of
God-forsakenness where the Son must go to seek and to save
that which is lost. But he does not remain there, and in his last
word, which echoes his first in the temple, he dies in peace and
confidence because God is still Abba.

In Gethsemane Abba was the one who had to be obeyed as
he made his unconditional demand; now he is the one who can
be trusted for the ultimate succour. The active obedience that
has given everything becomes passive trust that appeals all the
issues of the day – his own vindication as well as the world's
salvation – to the final court of appeal, who is Father, and
dies expecting his answer. The words are from the LXX of
Psalm 31.5 regularly used as a Jewish evening prayer, but here
with the all-significant Abba prefaced to it by Jesus. To die
knowing who you are, in the presence and power of Father is
already to take the sting from death – it is already to be
turned in hope towards the third day and the resurrection.
Those of us who have watched and helped our own loved ones
to die in that presence and confidence know what a mighty
thing it is – and can only pray that when our own time comes,
we also shall know Abba.

So, all the way from the boy in the temple to the man on the cross, at every critical point of temptation, decision, suffering and death, Jesus finds his identity and his confidence in his relationship to his Father and the obedience and trust with which he responds to it, and at each point of need God's fatherhood and his own sonship are freshly reaffirmed and revealed.

2 Jesus is dependent upon the Father, because it is the Father who reveals him and makes him known to others, just as it is the Son who makes the Father known to others. Just as the Son glorifies the Father, i.e. makes him known in his presence and power, so the Father bears witness to the Son (John 8.18) and glorifies the Son (John 8.54). In the words and works of Jesus, there is a reciprocal glorification of Father and Son.

It is interesting to note that both in Matthew and John there is a tendency to attribute to the Father the work of bringing people into recognition and confession of the mystery and person of Jesus, which is elsewhere attributed to the ministry of the Holy Spirit.

a So in Matthew 11.27, as we have seen, not only is exclusive knowledge of the Father attributed to the Son, but exclusive knowledge of the Son is attributed to the Father. The fundamental relationship is between Father and Son, and others are able to know one only through the activity of the other.

b More specifically, the insight that prompts Peter's confession of Jesus as Messiah and Son of God, which is typical of all Christian confession, is expressly attributed by Jesus to the action of the Father. "Blessed are you, Simon son of Jonah, for this was not revealed to you by man, but by my Father in heaven" (16.17). In I Corinthians 12.3 Paul ascribes what is basically an identical confession of Jesus as Lord to the work of the Holy Spirit. This involves no kind of contradiction, when we remember that the Holy Spirit is the executant of the Father's sovereign will in conveying his own truth, love and power to men.

c In John 6 Jesus is more than once careful to acknowledge the activity of the Father when men "come to him". He starts with the contrast between seeing and believing. All have seen him, but not all have believed (v.36). What is it that decides whether those who see Jesus will also believe in him (v.40), be drawn to him (v.44), come to him (v.65)? His own answer is that it is the Father who gives him disciples (v.37), who draws men (v.44), and enables them to come to him (v.65). When a man comes to or believes in Jesus, behind the human confession, following, discipleship, there is a divine selecting, revealing, enabling which Jesus recognises and proclaims. The action of the Father does not exclude or throw into question the necessity or genuineness of the human activity, but it precedes, enables and sustains it. The human choice has behind it the Father's choice, the human coming, the divine drawing, the human believing, God's revealing. Jesus is bound to receive all who come to him, because he knows that their coming does not have its origin either in him or in them, but in the Father, so that the obedient Son receives all whom the sovereign Father sends, "All that the Father gives me will come to me, and whoever comes to me I will never drive away" (v.37). The Father's sovereign will precedes, elicits and creates human choice, although it never abolishes or compels it. For Jesus the sign that God has been at work in men is that they come to him. "Everyone who listens to the Father and learns from him comes to me" (v.45).

Of course John himself can also speak of the Holy Spirit as performing this very function. In John 3.5 it is the Spirit who brings men to rebirth so that they can see and enter the kingdom. In John 16 it is the Spirit who takes the things of Jesus and shows them to us (16.15), and convinces the world of sin, righteousness and judgement (16.8). Even in 6.63 the communication of the life of Jesus to us is a work of the Holy Spirit. It is interesting to ask how these two ways of speaking of the same work of revelation and regeneration, as a work of the Father or as a work of the Spirit are related to each other. Several suggestions can be made.

i   In John there is already an incipient trinitarianism which
    knows that there is a basic unity between the action of the
    Father and the action of the Spirit so that there can be no hard
    and fast separation between them. The Spirit *is* the Father and
    the Son reaching out in communication and love beyond
    themselves towards another, so that the activity of revelation
    can rightly be attributed to each singly and all jointly.

ii There may be a temporal distinction involved here. Before
    the explicit emergence of the Spirit in the glorification of Jesus
    (John 7.39, 16.7), to which the main references to his work in
    the farewell discourses refer, what is afterwards known to be
    his work is first seen as the mysterious and sovereign work of
    the Father.

iii The Father and Spirit as joint revealers of the Son may remind
    us that in the coming of men to Christ there is a providential
    element which is outward, and a more strictly spiritual ele-
    ment which is inward. As the Father works outwardly, so the
    Spirit works inwardly to the same end. There is an openness to
    the gospel which is to some degree conditioned by outward
    circumstances. For example, a slave in ancient Rome is better
    placed outwardly to appreciate an offer of liberation in Christ
    than his master, so that more slaves than masters turned to
    Christ. On the other hand there is an inner openness which is
    in uncertain and ambiguous relationship to the outer; a man
    may be set in an outward situation where Christ can be easily
    and clearly seen, but whether he will in fact see and accept
    him is another, connected but different question. Donald
    McGavran in his writing on Church growth[6] has shown clearly
    that wherever there have been large scale conversions on the
    mission field, there have been a series of outward providential
    factors, e.g. among the Untouchables of India, that have
    predisposed certain kinds of people towards the gospel. One
    of the weaknesses of his work is that he tends to explain
    everything in these terms, even to the point of suggesting that
    if we could know fully all the external circumstances at work
    in a situation, we could predict or even perhaps engineer

revival. In other words he does not leave room for the properly spiritual factor, the mysterious blowing of the wind of the Spirit that impels a man into the kingdom and leaves another in precisely the same external situation outside it. So the outward ordering of circumstances and events by the Father and the inward and sovereign enlightening and regenerating action of the Spirit are related, but not identical factors in the making of Christians.

iv It may also be that John speaks of the Father when he is thinking of the sovereign source of God's revealing activity and of the Spirit when he is thinking of the immediate enabler of Christian decision. The Father's decree in heaven and the spiritual event here on earth are inseparable and indispensable parts of the one divine activity. There is no divine decree that is not worked out at some point by the Spirit in terms of actual human experience. And every activity of the Spirit has its source not in human decisions, techniques and persuasions, but is according to the will of the Father. He can be commanded and manipulated by none, but only prayed for in accordance with God's covenant and promise.

Whatever the relationship between the work of the Father and that of the Spirit, our main point here is that the revealing of Christ to men and the bringing of men to Christ involves a sovereign activity of the Father; it is he who glorifies his Son and makes him known.

3 Just as the will of the Father is executed through the Son as its essential agent, so the action of the Son is totally dependent upon and determined by the Father. Every action of Jesus originates and is directed by and towards the person, purpose and glory of the Father. It is from first to last *obedient* action, not initiating or innovating, but rather discerning and following. This is not a limitation on its spontaneity and freedom, but rather the source of it, because it is always personal response within a relationship and never external conformity to impersonal rule and regulation.

a The Father is the *source* of the Son's mission. Jesus is the *apostolos*, the one sent by the Father, who has a mission to fulfil that his Father has given to him. Hebrews 10.7 quoting the LXX of Psalm 40.8 identifies the central motivation, driving compulsion and energising purpose of his whole life and ministry, "I have come to do your will, O God." John 6.38 can stand for a whole multitude of Johannine texts that say the same thing, "I have come down from heaven not to do my own will but to do the will of him who sent me." At the end of the gospel he calls and integrates his disciples into the very same mission to which his Father has called him, "As the Father has sent me, I am sending you" (John 20.21).

b The action of the Father is in continual control of the action of the Son. There operates in the life of Jesus a secret, commanding and continuous personal guidance that shapes his decisions at every point. The source of his authority, as the believing Roman centurion recognised is that he was himself "a man under authority" (Luke 7.8) and it was always the authority of his Father. "I am telling you the truth that the Son can do nothing of his own; he does only what he sees the Father doing. What the Father does, the Son does also. For the Father loves the Son and shows him all that he himself is doing" (John 5.19–20). That is not simply a statement of theological principle but a description of the daily life of Jesus perhaps by someone who had shared it and knew all the listening, waiting and watching for what his Father was doing that filled its every part.

c The Father is the future of the Son's mission in the double sense that the completed work of the Son is submitted to the verdict of the Father, but also that he builds the kingdom not for himself but for the Father and, when it is completed, hands it over to the Father, "that God may be all in all" (I Corinthians 15.28). The subordination of the Son to the Father at the completion of the kingdom of which Paul speaks in that strange passage in I Corinthians 15 represents his sense of the priority of the Father. It all comes from him through Christ at the beginning; it all returns to him through Christ at the end. As it is put more simply in Philippians 2.10, when every tongue confesses the lordship of Jesus and every knee bows before his name, it is not for his own glory but "to the glory of God the Father". Thus the mission is *from* the Father as its initiating source, *with* the Father as its continuing authority, and *for* the Father as its ultimate purpose.

Is there anything rather more specific that we can say at this point about the way in which the Father guides the Son in his mission and shows him what he is doing? Is it so unique and hidden in the inner mysteries of the life of the holy Trinity from which we are for ever excluded, that the only course open to us is reverent and adoring silence?

Perhaps we can say rather more than that; there is indeed mystery here, but it is revealed mystery, mystery expressed under the conditions of incarnation. The unique communication of Father and Son in the Holy Spirit is now expressed in human form as the speaking of a man with his God. The way in which God guides Jesus is the same way in which God guides us, although the purpose and ministry into which he guides him is that appropriate to his eternal Son and so different from that into which he guides us. The commerce of Father and Son is translated into human terms, while still remaining itself, and as we read in and between the lines of the gospels we can trace something of the ways in which Father and Son in the glorious mystery of their being speak together.

a The Father shows the Son what he is doing, not mainly by obscure mystical illuminations, but in the context of human affairs and the events of the world around him. Jesus is wide open to the world and to all the activities of men; it is the cinema and the pulpit within which the Father shows him what he is doing. This is the basis of his teaching through parables. The sower and his seed, the shepherd and his lost sheep, the father and his two sons – these in themselves do not amount to revelation, but to him who has eyes to see and ears to hear, they are the language in which the Father is able to speak to his Son and through him to all his children.

Jesus came to see that his way was the way to the cross within the context of his understanding of the reaction of ordinary people, and especially of the Jewish religious authorities to him. As he sensitively discerned the needs and reactions that met him in the villages of Galilee, his Father showed him what awaited him in Jerusalem, and why it was only through death and resurrection that his purpose could be accomplished. If we do not know the world we live in, we shall never know what God wants to do with us in it; the word of the Father is spoken in connection with the people and events amidst which we live.

b His Father spoke to him out of the past tradition of his people, which had already been the place of God's action and self-revelation, for what God was about to do now was in continuity and fulfilment of what he had for long been doing in Israel, and that was recorded in its scriptures. What happened on the mount of transfiguration, when he communed with Moses and Elijah about his own exodus, was only an intensification of that dialogue with the law and the prophets in which Jesus heard his Father speak. He was steeped in scripture, as all his teaching shows; but he handled it with startling liberty and extraordinary boldness, as did his apostles after him. He came to see that the connection between Old Testament promise and his own fulfilment of it would be amazingly different from what anyone had ever imagined. That is why he handles the Old Testament with an authority quite different from that of the scribes, "It was said by those of old time, but I say to you" – and yet what he says is always the surprising consummation and fulfilment of what was said before.

He is integrally bound to scripture. Every time his Father is recorded as speaking to him it is in the words and echoes of the Old Testament; when he resists the temptations in the wilderness, when he defines his mission at Nazareth, when he institutes his supper and speaks both the words of dereliction and of trust upon the cross, it is all in fresh application of the ancient scriptures. The freshness of prophecy is always related to the givenness of the tradition from which it springs. The prophetic ministry of Jesus is quite original at many points, and yet at the same time it is so dependent upon the revelation of the past that it could not be understood without it. Every category in which he and those around him sought to understand him and his work, Son of Man, kingdom, Messiah, servant of God, makes sense only when we know both its scriptural origin and the new meaning that Jesus lives and dies into it. God's speaking to his Son and to his children through him is by the scriptures, and where they have no authority, neither will he.

c He prayed to his Father. Prayer became the means of the communication of the Son with the Father and of the answering communication of the Father with the Son. John is a little reluctant to admit to Jesus' dependence at least upon public prayer, and more than once explains that he did it for the sake of the people and not because he needed to for himself (e.g. John 11.42). Luke on the other hand carefully notes how he made time with God priority right through his ministry, especially where there were great decisions immediately ahead. The prayer of Jesus about which we know most is his prayer in Gethsemane and we can see in it factors that almost certainly marked all his secret dealings with his Father.

Jesus begins that prayer with a *confession* – not of his sin, but of his situation and of his own desire about it, namely that the cup of suffering should be allowed to pass from him. There is no pious concealing of what he wants; he makes his desires known very freely and realistically, and yet at the same time his desire is submitted to his Father's will. The Son does not thrust his will on the Father on the pretext that he can ask for anything or "claim in faith" whatever he likes.

There is also a *discerning* of his Father's will. As he goes on praying in great agony, he comes to see more and more clearly that what he began by asking cannot be given to him, but that what his Father is doing requires that he drink the cup to its bitter dregs. He only does what he sees the Father doing and as he prays in the garden he sees the Father undertaking a redemption which can be achieved only by his own sacrifice, and therefore he attunes his will again to his Father, "If this cup cannot pass from me unless I drink it, Abba, not my will but yours be done."

When his Father's will is grasped the atmosphere changes, the agony is over and he rises calm and brave to proceed. Here we see how at the central climax of his life Jesus discerned in prayer what his Father was doing, but he could do this in Gethsemane only because he has been doing the same thing in less extreme situations all his days.

d Through living in the world, through scripture, through prayer, there comes to Jesus again and again a particular grasp of the Father's specific will for a particular situation. He acts in his dealings with people in healing and pastoral encounter not by rule or according to principle, but rather situationally and creatively, in a way that is adapted to the special person or trouble that confronts him. This is the action of the Holy Spirit by whom God gives his truth, his love, and his power not in general and in the abstract, but in a way that is uniquely relevant to the present situation. Jesus has again and again in the Spirit a particular seeing and hearing of what his Father wants to do at this very place and at this very moment. He acts not by employing a method or a technique or by "applying Christian principles" but by charismatic insight that has the sensitivity to see what God is doing here and now. His specific grasp of God's will is the picture and the promise of the discernment into which the Spirit seeks to lead his people.

These are the ways in which the Son discerns the Father's will and obeys it. The final expression of the Son's dependence upon the Father is of course in his death and resurrection. Just as the Father is the past from which he comes, and the present in which he lives, so also specially in the cross he is the future to which he goes. The resurrection is the Father's verdict upon his Son's perfected obedience, the reversal *in toto* of the various hostile verdicts of Rome and Israel, of state and church, of foe and friend. It is the reversal of the past and the inauguration of the future, it is the anticipation of the final judgement, the firstfruits and promise of the new heaven and the new earth. As the central act of history it is the chief work of the Father. The verbs that describe it are in regard to the Son characteristically passive, but in regard to the Father gloriously active, "Blessed be the God and Father of our Lord Jesus Christ. In his great mercy he has given us new birth into a living hope through the resurrection of Jesus Christ from the dead" (I Peter 1.3). This is indeed the Father's characteristic blessedness that when the Son went the whole way of obedience, his Father in whom he trusted raised him from the dead.

1 Dietrich Bonhoeffer; *Letters and Papers from Prison* (Enlarged Edition S.C.M. 1967) p 348.
2 Alex Haley *Roots* (Pan Books 1977).
3 Norman Anderson *The Mystery of the Incarnation* (Hodder & Stoughton 1978) p 16.
4 Louis Bouyer *Le Fils Eternal* (Paris, Cerf 1974) p 510 quoted by Anderson, op. cit. p 17.
5 I. Howard Marshall *The Gospel of Luke* (Paternoster 1978) ad loc.
6 Donald McGavran *Understanding Church Growth* (Eerdmans 1970).

Chapter Five

God the Father and God the Son

Our last two chapters have been in effect an extended exposition of Matthew 11.27. There is no knowledge of the Father except through the Son; there is no knowledge of the Son except through the Father. But precisely at this point another and indeed the crucial question in this whole area inevitably arises. Is it enough to say what we have been saying up till now, that Jesus is the means by which we know God, or do we have to go beyond that and say that in some sense Jesus is himself God? Is Jesus of Nazareth only the historical means by which God delivered his people and in so doing made himself known? Does he therefore belong to the dispensable super-structure of revelation and salvation? Or does his relationship with his Father belong to the life of God from all eternity, so that God is God only as this Father and this Son in this relationship to one another? Orthodox Christianity with its doctrines of incarnation and Trinity has chosen the second of these alternatives, but in our day there are many who are saying that the New Testament gospel is hindered and encumbered, rather than elucidated and clarified by the dead-weight that these ancient doctrinal formulations have imposed upon it. For effective evangelism in the modern world we need to set our statements about Christ in his work free from the artificial and unnecessary difficulties that they impose. This discussion of the continuing adequacy and indeed necessity of the doctrine of the incarnation is at the centre of contemporary theological discussion. Our answers to the vital and central questions about the person and work of Christ that it raises, will shape for good or ill the whole future of the Church's life and mission.

Into that discussion we are now to some extent bound to enter. We must do so briefly and not too technically, keeping our attention on the main issues involved rather than the detailed questions raised by the work of particular scholars. Also we must keep our eyes on our own particular concern and not allow ourselves to be diverted too far from it. Our question is, what is the significance, status and nature of the Father/Son relationship? Is it the *means* of revelation and salvation or, more than that, is it the *content* of revelation and salvation? Is the God who speaks to and saves us the Father who acts *through* Jesus, or is he the one who shows himself in the midst of human history as divine Father and divine Son because that is what he is in himself from all eternity?

Many modern theologians, dissatisfied with the traditional formulations of Trinity and incarnation, and of a more or less radical turn of mind, have laid emphasis on what has come to be called a *functional* view of the person and work of Christ. We need to concentrate on what Jesus did, and not ask basically irrelevant questions about who Jesus was. He is the *means* by which God does his work of revelation and salvation among us, very much as Moses was the means by whom God delivered his people from Egypt and showed himself to them. While it makes sense to say that Moses was of the greatest historical importance functionally in that it was through him that God spoke and acted, it is obviously unnecessary and, to put it mildly, inappropriate to say that God's relationship to Moses is in any way constitutive of his own divine being and nature.

While of course God's action in Christ is much more fundamental and universal than his action in Moses, Christologies of this kind would hold that there is no difference in principle between the relationship that God had with the two men through whom he acted. They describe Jesus almost exclusively in terms of his function in revelation. He is the mirror in which God has reflected himself in a human life, or alternatively he is the window through which we can see into the heart and being of God and his purposes.

Now the mirror of the telescope is a necessary means for our seeing of the star, but it is in no sense part of the star that we look at. The window is the necessary access to the world outside the room, which apart from it would be invisible, but the window is not part of the view, and to concentrate too much on the window is to be distracted from the view.

As we have seen, the New Testament does indeed want to say that Jesus is functionally necessary in this way. He is the image of the invisible God, and the way by which we know the Father. Some theologians who adopt this kind of approach (e.g. John Robinson) would maintain that Jesus is uniquely necessary for the revelation of God, that he is not one of many telescopes trained on the distant divine star or one of many alternative mirrors of the Father's truth and love, but the one and indispensable means that God has chosen to make himself normatively and finally known among us.

But the key word is *means* – Jesus performs a function, an indispensable function it may be in revelation and salvation. As a result all we need fundamentally say about the Father and the Son is that the former speaks and works through the latter, as his mirror, his mouthpiece, his agent. This functional language can say adequately all that the New Testament wants to say about Jesus (or perhaps all that it *should* want to say!). If we go beyond it into the traditional language of incarnation we shall throw into doubt the real humanity of Jesus and his identity with us, and involve ourselves in the completely superfluous and, to modern man incredible, mythology of a pre-existent divine Son who in a unique act of supernatural intervention took upon himself human flesh.

We may readily grant to such a functional view of the relationship of Jesus to God the merits of simplicity when compared for example with the complicated categories of the Christology of Chalcedon. We should, however, also remember that the Christology of Chalcedon was formulated, not out of any love for philosophical speculation, but precisely because the Church had learned the hard way over the pre-

ceding centuries, that simplicity in Christology can be purchased far too expensively if it is destructive of the heart of the
gospel.

We are therefore driven back to the New Testament itself
and to the question whether what it says about Jesus can be
adequately expressed in functional terms. H. E. W. Turner,
in discussing John Robinson's Christology which is of this
type, makes a valid general point. "There is an important
scholastic principle that 'operation follows being' (*operari
sequitur esse*). This calls attention to the need to offer an
adequate ontological grounding for unity in activity and operation. The functional cannot replace the ontological as the
final target for Christology. Penultimate concerns cannot be
substituted for the ultimate questions that insist on raising
their heads. Despite his obvious intention to the contrary,
Robinson seems to be working a dimension short through his
rejection of the supernaturalist frame and his refusal to push
beyond the functional to the ontological in Christology"[1].

To put that more simply, verbs require subjects. The function that somebody performs inevitably raises questions about
the nature and status of the person who performs it. If it is
claimed that the works of Jesus are the works of God, we have
inevitably to ask what that means, and what implications the
nature of his works have for the nature of his person. Can a man
do the work of God in the sense that Jesus is said to do it, and not
be God? Such a question is an ontological one (it has to do
with the being and not just the work of Jesus), and Turner is
surely right in saying that it cannot simply be ruled out of court
by a refusal to go beyond what is strictly functional.

Let us therefore put this question to the New Testament by
asking in the first place what the gospel of John means when it
attributes to Jesus the statement about his relationship to his
Father in John 10.30, "I and the Father are one." Many
modern commentators follow the functionalist exegesis of
Bultmann in his commentary on the gospel (p 295 E.T.), who
holds that the passage asserts a moral unity between the words
and acts of Jesus and those of God. In will, purpose and act,
the Father and I are one. That at any rate was not the way his

claim was understood by his Jewish hearers, whose ears were much more ontologically tuned than those of Bultmann, so that they accused him of blasphemy "because you, a mere man, claim to be God" (v.33). Jesus does not repudiate that claim but simply asks them whether his words substantiate it and establish him as God's Son (v.36) and "the one whom the Father set apart as his very own and sent into the world" (v.36).

Many of the commentators (Barrett, Temple, Hoskyns and Davy)[2] point out that the language of the gospel at this point is not to be understood metaphysically. The interest here is as always intensely practical and concretely theological – concerned with God. But the right contrast here is not between the practical and the metaphysical, as if the latter meant the irrelevantly theoretical and abstractly speculative. The contrast is between practical and concrete statements about the action and function of Jesus, and equally practical and concrete statements about the being of Jesus and its relationship to the being of the Father. The "being" statements may prove as practical as the "doing" statements if it can be established that the gospel cannot be fully stated without them.

There is nothing speculative or philosophical about John 10.30 any more than there is anything speculative or philosophical about the prologue to the gospel in John 1. Both make practical and necessary theological statements about the relationship of the Word or Son to the Father, because they believe that such statements are necessary presuppositions for the whole New Testament gospel. That is why it is perfectly legitimate to understand the one in relation to the other. Behind the unity of will, purpose and action between Jesus and his Father which the gospel everywhere affirms, there is the unity of being between God and his Word, and there is no reason to doubt that it is that unity of being, as the basis for the unity of action between himself and his Father, that Jesus is claiming in John 10.30, especially since the discussion that follows in the rest of the chapter makes sense only on that assumption, as we have seen. "When I speak, my Father speaks, when I act, my Father acts, my action is his action also, because we share together in the one divine life, being and nature."

But what is there about the gospel that requires us to follow John in asserting this very difficult notion of a divine being, nature, identity, that is shared by the Father in heaven and Jesus as man on earth? Why will the simpler notion of agreement in speech and action between God and the man Jesus not do just as well? There are three ways in which an answer to that question may be given.

a The correspondence in will and action between God and Jesus can be explained by saying that Jesus is of all men the one most inspired by God; whereas the divine identity between Jesus and his Father can be explained only by saying that Jesus is the incarnation of God. It is the difference between the indwelling of the Spirit and the enfleshing of the Word, between the witness of the prophet and the witness of the Son.

If we remain within the realm of inspiration and of the work of the Holy Spirit in a human life, then the boundary and distinction between the inspirer and the inspired, the giver and the receiver remains intact. When I am inspired by the Holy Spirit, he works in me, but in such a way that I do not become the Holy Spirit, nor does the Holy Spirit become me. Each remains himself, and the value of the relationship consists in the fact that it is between a divine will and a separate human will that has been brought into obedient correspondence to it, but the two remain two, however close the interaction between them.

Thus when the inspired prophet says, "Thus says the Lord", he does not mean that his speaking is identical with God's speaking because his person has become identical with God's person, but only that a functional and very possibly temporary correspondence of content has been established between his word and God's word by God's Spirit, so that his word is a true and valid witness to the word of God, for as long as the Spirit goes on inspiring, and he yields to that inspiration.

But the formula on the lips of Jesus is not the prophetic "Thus says the Lord" but the quite distinct and different "Verily, I say to you". His word is not God's word occasionally when by the action of the Holy Spirit what he says as man corresponds to the word of God; his word is God's word from the very fact that he says it, out of the personal divine authority that he both receives from his Father but also shares with him. In the works and words of Jesus there is an identity between the divine source of the action and its human agent, that carries us not to a higher degree of inspiration but out of the category of inspiration altogether, where inspirer and inspired are always two, into the realm of incarnation where the human agent is in fundamental identity with the divine source of his action and acts and speaks not as inspired man only, but as an inspiring God. Thus when Jesus says that "My Father and I are one", he does not abolish the distinction between them, but he does assert an identity between them that is quite different in nature from the functional correspondence in word and action between prophet and God, or even between the Christian and the abiding Holy Spirit.

That is why the way in which Jesus asserted his authority as one who was able to do what only God could do again and again gave rise to a charge of blasphemy against him. In Matthew Jesus is the authoritative interpreter of the Mosaic law. "It was said of them of old time, but I say to you" (Matthew 5 *passim*). That authority is of course the Father's but it is one asserted here directly, immediately and personally by Jesus as one who has divine right to do so. In Mark his claim to be able to forgive sins is of such a direct and immediate kind that it immediately raises the question, "Why does this fellow talk like this? He's blaspheming. Who can forgive sins but God alone?" (Mark 2.7). The assumption that only God can forgive sins is not challenged by what Jesus says in reply. Instead the right of the Son of Man to do what only God can do is validated by the healing ministry that follows. He does not point away from himself to God's authority, as does a prophet; he exercises it as one who has the right to do so.

So also in John 5.17 when Jesus says, "My Father is always at his work to this very day and I am working too" is immediately understood as "calling God his own Father, making himself equal to God" (v.18), when in fact it could quite well mean merely he is doing his own divine work and I am doing my human work as his obedient and responsive servant. That was not however what his hearers heard, but the claim to be a second divine agent alongside the Father in the performance of the divine work.

As has often been pointed out, that becomes even more explicit in the Johannine "I am" sayings, where Jesus claims to be in his way, no less than the Father in his different way, the source of truth and life.

The ontological identity of Jesus with God in John's gospel becomes quite explicit after the resurrection when the final word is spoken by Thomas that takes us beyond all functional Christology to a recognition of Jesus as the one to whom with the Father no less than worship is due, "Thomas answered, 'My Lord and my God!'" (20.28). One does not worship the mirror or the window, the prophet or even the Spirit-filled Christian. The distinction between the one who inspires and the other who is inspired remains in all these cases intact and inviolate. If Jesus is only the man who shows us God, then our worship belongs not to him but only to the God whom he shows us.

On such a functional assumption the universal attribution of the divine name *Kurios*, Lord, to Jesus by the Christian tradition at its earliest stage seems quite inexplicable. Despite the cavillings of radical New Testament critics, the argument seems to me still to stand that in calling Jesus *kurios* and in making that attribution the primary Christian confession, these men, brought up in the strictest Jewish monotheism, made nothing less than an ontological identification between their crucified and risen master and the God of Israel who sent him, with all the implications for worship that that implied. In Revelation the throne of God has become the throne of God and of the Lamb, and for Paul equally, at his name every knee is to bow and every tongue confess precisely that he is *Kurios*, and this acknowledgement of his divine status is not to the despite but precisely to the glory of God the Father.

It is of course perfectly possible to demythologise the New Testament gospel in order to make it less 'metaphysical' and so more acceptable to the needs of modern man and, as part of this process, to assign Jesus only the role that a functional theology thinks adequate; but it is difficult to hold either that such a functional Jesus is the subject of the original New Testament witness, or that the revised gospel, that will be consistent with such a reconstituted Jesus, will have any real resemblance to the gospel it replaces.

Our present point is that the gospel as given requires not just a functionally inspired Jesus, but one who is in ontological identity with his Father as the incarnate Son.

b   Functional views of the relationship between Jesus and God go happily together with interpretations of the work of Jesus which see it mainly in terms of revelation. His words and deeds point beyond themselves to the truth, love and power of God to which they bear witness. His cross is the climax of that revelation, an enacted assertion of his love to the world, which manifests his relationship to men rather than changes it. If, however, we see God not so much as the object of revelation, but rather as the subject of salvation, who intervenes decisively in his Son to change the whole human and cosmic situation, then the question about the identity of Jesus as the agent of that intervention and change acquires a new urgency. Sir Norman Anderson makes almost the same point, "Those who insist on a Christology which regards Christ as exclusively human, even if the locus or agent of a uniquely divine revelatory event, take a subjective rather than objective view of the atonement – or, to be more precise, a view which concentrates on the subjective effect on man of what they would certainly accept as an objective event. Those of us, on the other hand, who regard the atonement as a fundamental importance, not only because of the subjective change it can, should, and does effect in man and his attitude to God, but also because it provides the essential basis on which alone a holy God can and does proffer a full and free forgiveness to the repentant sinner – free to him because the God who proffers it has redeemed him at so great a cost – must necessarily, I believe, find this Christology inadequate"[3].

The biblical diagnosis of the human situation is that because of sin the relationship of the world with God has fallen into all sorts of disarray, and that the judgement of his wrath lies against it, so that there is need of a drastic and effective act of reconciliation. If we accept that diagnosis, the question about the identity of the agent of that reconciliation becomes of the first importance. How can the act of atonement on the cross be reconciling, effective, creative and of universal import for all men, unless the agent of it is himself God? In the New Testament salvation and reconciliation are supremely the act of God himself in his grace, and their effectiveness stems largely from that fact. "God was reconciling the world to himself in Christ, not counting men's sins against them" (II Corinthians 5.19).

If we take this merely functionally to mean that God was inspiring the obedient man Jesus Christ to reconcile the world to himself, then one's whole confidence in the reality of the reconciliation he has effected begins to fade. What is this grace of God that at the crucial point does not come himself or give himself, but sends another? How could any man, however inspired or obedient, effect what Jesus is here said to have effected – the reconciliation of the world with God. One could understand how the death of an inspired and obedient Jesus might be a sign of God's will for reconciliation, but how could it be its effective enactment (v.18), the setting aside of sin, the beginning of the rule of righteousness (v.21), the inauguration of a new creation (v.17), all of which is affirmed of it here?

Paul's presupposition here is that all these things can be affirmed of the cross if it is seen to be in the strongest possible sense the work of God himself, as indeed he says, "From first to last this has been the work of God" (v.18). Any Christological weakness at this decisive point must have the effect of throwing into doubt the real involvement of God himself with the salvation of the world, and therefore the reality of his grace and of the effect of what was done. The divine initiative and involvement can be preserved only by a theology that identifies the author and the agent of the reconciliation, as sharing in their different ways, as Father and Son, in a divine authority, creativity and identity. The action of Jesus, as man among us and for us, has universal significance only if it is also the action of God, if God was indeed in Christ as man on the cross reconciling the world to himself.

The same high Christology is implied in Colossians, "For God was pleased to have all his fulness dwell in him, and through him to reconcile to himself all things, whether things on earth or things in heaven by making peace through his blood shed on the cross" (Colossians 1.20). Here again Christology is the presupposition of effective atonement.

So also in Galatians. "But when the time had fully come, God sent his Son (*ton huion autou*), born of a woman, born under law, to redeem those under law" (4.4). This is not a sending in which the one who sends remains behind, it is a sending of himself in his Son which makes the whole action from beginning to end significant as the action of God himself. So in John 3.16 he who is given is "his only begotten Son" (*ton huion ton monogene*), with the implication that in giving his Son God gave himself for us. What is at stake here is not merely an ultimate revelation of God's love, for which an inspired man might arguably have been adequate, but the reversal of the human condition from a state of perishing to one of eternal life.

When we are bid to eat of bread that is his broken body and drink of blood that inaugurates the new covenant, our confidence in what we do depends upon the answer to the question whose body and whose blood it is that we take, and the only adequate answer is that it is the body and blood of the Son of God who loved me and gave himself for me and in so doing brought to the rescue the very wisdom, power and love of the Father, so that the atoning obedience that reconciled us was the obedience of God offered as man for all men.

Where we see the need of the world in less urgent terms, a

functional Christology and a revelatory atonement may suffice, but when, with the New Testament witnesses, we see ourselves as those "who were dead in your trespasses and sins" (Ephesians 2.1) and "without hope and without God in the world" (2.13), we shall not find it so hard to appreciate that it takes a sending by God the Father which involves a coming of God the Son to put this right, an action that is not only inspired by God, but in which God himself acts. The old insight of Anselm still stands; our Christology is not determined primarily by our philosophy, but by our estimation of our plight and what it took to cope with it – *quantum ponderis peccatum* (how mighty was our sin).

c Basically the same comment can be made about Christologies which attempt to speak about Christ more directly in relation to the Holy Spirit, as *the* Spirit-filled man *par excellence*. Such a Christology has been worked out carefully and subtly by G. W. Lampe[4], and the same general approach is characteristic of D. M. Baillie[5] even though he seeks to interpret Jesus as the man full of grace rather than the man filled with the Spirit, and is characteristically offering a reinterpretation of the old Christological approach rather than, with Lampe, a replacement of it.

We have already to a certain extent responded to this sort of Christology in our discussion of the relationship between inspiration and incarnation, but there are two other considerations that can now be usefully added. The first is that the New Testament itself fails almost totally to give any support for an attempt to interpret the person of Jesus in terms of *Pneuma*, Spirit. As Professor Moule tellingly remarks, "The virtual non-attribution of the term spirit to Jesus is . . . startling. Whereas the Wisdom literature had used *logos* and *sophia* and *pneuma*, if not as interchangeable terms, at least in the closest conjunction, the New Testament almost consistently reserves *pneuma* for the activity of God among Christians *through* Christ rather than applying it to Christ himself . . . The appropriation of *logos* and *sophia* but rejection of *pneuma* for Jesus seems (for whatever reason) to be something decidedly distinctive of the Christian response to events"[6]. However helpful or enlightening a Spirit Christology may be in the contemporary situation it cannot look for much explicit encouragement from the New Testament original.

I would want to argue in addition that the category of Spirit-filled Man is inadequate to comprehend all that the New Testament wants to say about Jesus and the Spirit. In his humanity he was indeed exactly that, the man in whom the Spirit dwelt without measure (John 3.34). That fact is of the greatest importance in understanding Christologically the work of the Spirit in us, as I tried to show in *Reflected Glory*.

But Jesus is more than Spirit-filled man, because the Spirit-filled man is completely and absolutely the recipient of the Spirit and never the disposer or controller of the Spirit. But the authority to dispense and dispose of the Spirit to others belongs to Jesus. John the Baptist, himself a man full of the Spirit – distinguishes himself from Jesus precisely on the ground that Jesus is able to impart the Spirit to others and John is not: "I baptise you with water. But one more powerful than I will come, the thongs of whose sandals I am not worthy to untie. He will baptise you with the Holy Spirit and with fire" (Luke 3.16). In John 1.33 these two aspects of Jesus' relation to the Spirit, as both human recipient and as divine bestower are held together. The speaker is again John, "He who sent me to baptise with water told me; The man on whom you see the Spirit come down and remain is he who will baptise with the Holy Spirit. I have seen and testify that this is the Son of God." We may compare this with the call of Jesus to thirsty men to come to him and drink of the Spirit as of living waters (John 7.37–39), and his promise in John 16.7, "I will send him to you."

The status of Christ as the source of the Spirit along with the Father is affirmed in the Western *Filioque* clause of the Creed of Nicaea, which, because it has such strong biblical backing, should not be lightly abandoned. Jesus is baptiser in the Spirit not simply as Spirit-filled man, for this, as we have seen, is the one thing that no Spirit-filled man is capable of doing. He sends and gives the Spirit as one who does what the Father does, because in his identity with the Father, he is the source of the Spirit. This is made clear in John 16.7 where the sending of the Spirit is seen to be dependent upon the work of Jesus and to be the prerogative of Jesus, not of course in competition with the Father, but in sovereign co-ordination with him, "Unless I go away, the Counsellor will not come to you; but if I go *I will send him.*" So also after the ascension and Pentecost Peter affirms that Jesus has received from the Father the sovereign authority to dispense the Holy Spirit to others, "He . . . has poured out what you now see and hear" (Acts 2.33). This places Jesus in a different category from that of the Spirit-filled man; it is not just that he has more of the Spirit than others, but that he does what only God can do and gives him to others. The Holy Spirit is the Spirit of Christ, because he is the normative archetype of life in the Spirit, but also because he is the source from whom the Spirit comes. In the same way the grace of God is also the grace of the Lord Jesus Christ, not just because he is supremely the man of grace, but because as the Son of the Father he confers that grace upon men.

To sum up thus far, the nature of the authority of Jesus, the effectiveness of his atoning work, his ability to confer the Holy Spirit upon others, require us to see him in a relationship with God that is not simply functional, involving his action, but that is also ontological, involving his being. Operation implies being, a verb requires an appropriate subject. In order to do what the gospel affirms that he does, he needs to be the one that the gospel affirms that he is. He needs to be not only a man brought by the Holy Spirit into inner and outer conformity with the mind, will, speech and action of God but one who stands in ontological identity with God, who acts as only God can act, and therefore is what only God can be, the Son of God and the Word of God.

The prologue to St John's gospel, far from being speculative or philosophical in intention, uses and reshapes to its own purposes the *Logos* (Word) language of its day to say what needs to be said to give the coming and saving activity of Jesus the one context in which it can be understood and grasped. "These things are written that you may believe that Jesus is the Christ, the Son of God, and that by believing you may have life in his name" (20.31), clearly indicates the evangelical intention of the prologue as of the whole gospel, as it seeks to describe one who is not the Father and who yet is God and as such has been with God from the beginning. It is such a one and no other who has been made flesh for our salvation, so that his word is in the most direct sense God's word, his truth God's truth, his Spirit God's Spirit.

Whenever the New Testament writers stand back a little from the immediacy of the events that define and fill their mission and reflect upon them in the light of the resurrection, this is the verdict about Jesus towards which, from their different standpoints and expressed in their different languages, they are driven. In Hebrews 1, where the *Logos* language is not used, the divine grandeur of Christ is as clearly affirmed as in John 1. "He has spoken to us by his Son, whom he appointed heir of all things and through whom he made the universe. The Son is the radiance of God's glory and the exact representation of his being (*character tes hupostaseos autou*), sustaining all things by his powerful word" (Hebrews 1.2–3). It is equally clear in the juxtaposition of the quotations from the psalms that follow, where Christ is contrasted with the angels (with whom God had a functional relationship!) as a divine Son. "But about the Son he says, 'Your throne, O God, will last for ever and ever'" (Psalm 45.6–7). This is ontological language with a vengeance, again not deployed in any speculative interest, but only to show how great is the salvation that has come among us (2.3) since it is God himself who announces it and executes it through the Son whom he acclaims with his own divine name.

What needs to be said about these prologues to John and Hebrews, needs to be said also about the doctrine of Christ's pre-existence which they contain, and which regularly recurs whenever the New Testament speaks about creation. Recreation in Christ is to be understood on the presupposition that creation itself was in Christ; he who has begun to remake everything is the one through whom everything was made.

How we regard the doctrine of pre-existence depends upon our fundamental stance in relation to the Christological questions we have been discussing. For a functional Christology, which has much in common with the adoptionism of the early centuries, Jesus is the man through whom God chose to act at the climax of his saving activity, so that any talk about his pre-existence is at best an irrelevant piece of speculation and at worst a real question mark against the reality of his humanity and his solidarity with the rest of mankind.

Typical of much modern Christology of this kind is the saying of John Knox which has been much quoted, "We can have the humanity without the pre-existence, and we can have the pre-existence without the humanity. There is absolutely no way of having both"[7]. The impossibility is not perhaps quite as absolute as Knox imagines. New Testament Christology and the classical Christian tradition have always thought that they could have both, so that it requires more than the say-so of Professor Knox to convince us not merely that they have not fully articulated the relationship between humanity and pre-existence, but that they are attempting to hold together two essentially incompatible concepts. Second, the incompatibility only arises when Knox and others who think in the same way convert the necessary assertion that Christ is a man as much as we are, and indeed that he is not less but more fully human than any of us, into the very dubious proposition that in order to be man, he cannot be anything else but man, and therefore cannot be God's pre-existent Son without at the same time ceasing to be man. The subtle change from "truly human" into "nothing but human", from "one with us in our manhood" to "in no way different from us in any other respect" of course excludes by definition any affirmation of the true divinity of Christ that goes beyond his manhood. It rules out of court the central mystery of the incarnation which Chalcedon defined even if it could not explain, that he is true man and true God, and that he can be the one without ceasing to be the other. There are all sorts of fruitful lines in which the relationship of humanity and divinity in the person of Christ are being discussed in current Christology, and to disqualify them all at one stroke by a dictum like Knox's is far from being the sum of wisdom that it may at first appear.

Whether the mystery of the incarnation, of Christ's true divinity and humanity, is a bogus one or a real one cannot be decided by juggling with concepts like humanity and pre-existence and defining one so that it excludes the other, but only be exposing ourselves to the given fact of Christ and asking if we can do justice to his person and work by saying of him any less than that he is truly God and truly man.

If, for the kinds of reasons we have been considering in this chapter, we affirm his ontological identity with God, then of course his pre-existence as divine Son follows from it, not as an extra piece of information about Jesus or as an invitation to speculate about his pre-incarnate life, but simply as a recognition that the relationship between Father and Son that expresses itself in human terms and under human conditions in the incarnation did not come into being with the birth of Jesus in Bethlehem, but belongs to the very life of God from eternity to eternity. God without his Son would not be the same God; his relationship with Christ is the relationship that constitutes his own life as God; the love between Jesus and his Father is the very love that is the source of creation and in the heart of the Creator. God did not acquire a Son at some stage in his history (as the Arians affirmed "there was a time when he was not"); the Son was *monogenes* – of his own being and nature.

What God did acquire in the incarnation of his Son was humanity in every way like ours, except that it was his and not ours, God's humanity. What was new and marvellous, full of grace and truth, was that for us men and our salvation he was made man, that the intercourse of Father and Son in the Holy Spirit which was eternal, was now without ceasing to be what it had always been, expressed in earthly and human form in the intercourse between Jesus of Nazareth and his heavenly Father in the same Holy Spirit. In this coming among us the relationship between Father and Son which was the basis of all relationship, that mutual giving that was the meaning of all love, that personal knowing that was the centre of all knowledge, was opened up to us and took our human life into itself, and so brought about our reconciliation, our sonship and our salvation. This is what we are saying when we speak about the pre-existence of the Word. We simply spell out what was implied from the beginning when we gave him the divine name and confessed that Jesus is *Kurios*, Lord. This is not to solve all the questions about his pre-existence and humanity, but it is to show why they are questions that have a basis in reality and not logical conundrums.

In discussing his pre-existence we have already implied a large part of what is contained in the doctrine of the Trinity, since the two are in the closest connection. The doctrine of the Trinity does not lay an irreverent philosophical mystery on top of a simple scriptural gospel; it simply makes explicit what is implicit in the biblical gospel, in order to defend it against precisely the philosophical attacks that are made upon it. The root of the doctrine of the Trinity is the same insight that in Jesus we have to do with one who is not only on our side as creature, but on God's side as Creator. He is of one being (*homousios*) with the Father and so belongs to God's life and not only to ours, but he brings his relationship with the Father into earthly revelation and action for our salvation. The doctrine of the Trinity resists all attempts to demote Christ from his divinity (Arianism and adoptionism), to impugn the reality and ultimacy of the relationship between Father and Son (modalism, Sabellianism) and insists that the unity of the Godhead and the reality of the relationships, within it are both essential constituents of the biblical gospel and of the life of the God who is revealed in it.

In maintaining the truth of the immanent or essential Trinity, it holds that the God who has come in his Son and worked in his Spirit is the only God that there is. From eternity to eternity he is the Father of the Lord Jesus Christ who loves and is loved by his Son in the unity of the Holy Spirit. There is no more absolute or ultimate deity behind him, no philosophical concept, ancient or modern, to which he has to be subordinated and so robbed of his deity. He is God and he alone. It is that affirmation of the doctrine of the Trinity that is still the best defence of the gospel against the attacks of whatever the prevailing philosophy of the day may be.

To recapitulate at this point, we have seen that the claim of the Johannine Christ "The Father and I are one" taken in the context of the whole gospel points on towards an identity of divine being between the Father in heaven and the Son on earth. The person and work of Christ stand on the divine as well as on the human side of reality, and the relationship between them constitutes the very life of God and is the basic presupposition of all his work of creation and redemption. When we stand with Jesus in Gethsemane and are, in the Holy Spirit, alive and awake to all that is going on there, we find ourselves not only at the holy heart of the life and being of the man Jesus in his prayer to Abba from the hour of his agony, but through the mirror of his suffering humanity we are looking right into the central secret of the universe, into the heart of God where Father and Son express in endless richness their mutual self-giving, the one to the other.

It is of the essence of God to be Father and Son, and the nature of this relationship determines everything else. In this relationship creation and all its structures and multiplicity of relationships, redemption and all its way of sacrifice and resurrection, family, state, the whole universe of human inter-relatedness find their ultimate significance. This Father and this Son in this Spirit are Creator, Preserver, Redeemer of it all. The central secret of the Christian life is that we are adopted into this relationship as children of this Father whose standing with him is both normatively expressed and sovereignly enabled by the coming of the Son into our humanity as our brother. All renewal in the Holy Spirit is essentially a renewal of this sonship, and the sign that this basic renewal is authentic is that all other relationships within the various contexts of life begin to be renewed as well.

Any concept of renewal which is smaller than that, and that concentrates on individual experiences of the Holy Spirit and his gifts in and for themselves is just too small. The work of the Spirit is defined by the fact that in it the Father calls us into a sharing of life with himself and his Son (I John 1.3). The day of renewal is that day of which Jesus spoke in John 14.20–21, "On that day you will realise that I am in my Father, and you are in me and I am in you. Whoever has my commands and obeys them, he is the one who loves me. He who loves me will be loved by my Father, and I too will love him and show myself to him."

Having stressed the central nature of the Father/Son relationship for our understanding of the gospel, we now have to go on and define it more carefully. So far we have been emphasising almost exclusively the divine identity of Father and Son, their sharing of one being and nature; but we have now to define more precisely what sort of relationship they have within the identity that they share. It is God who stands at both ends of the relationship – that is what we have said so far – and to that extent it is mutual or reciprocal. But that is not all that is to be said about it. As we defined the identity by one Johannine word of Jesus, so now we describe the nature of the relationship by another, "The Father is greater than I" (John 14.28).

This also has a context in the entire gospel and indeed in the New Testament as a whole. Jesus while he shares the divine authority that we have already described and acts as God, because he is God, nevertheless insists that he is second and the Father first. What he says is what he has first learned from the Father, what he does is what he has first seen the Father doing. He has come, as we have already seen, not to do his own will but the will of him that sent him. When we spoke of the dependence of Jesus upon the Father we saw that it was a dependence that expressed itself in obedience; the Father initiated, Jesus executed, the Father sent, the Son came, the Father purposed, the Son obeyed.

If we were talking only about the man Jesus, such a relationship of obedience to God would be almost taken for granted as exemplary and appropriate to all godly men. But if we take seriously the divine identity of Jesus, another problem and possibility arises. Can we talk of a divine obedience? Is there in God an ability not just to be first and command, but also to be second and obey? Is there within the one life of God a real subordination of the divine Son to the divine Father? Can we really say with Karl Barth that "for God it is just as natural to be lowly as it is to be high, to be near as it is to be far, to be little as it is to be great, to be abroad as it is to be at home"?[8].

Barth, on whose exposition we are dependent at this point, goes on to make it clear that this notion of a divine obedience is a difficult one, "It is a difficult and even an elusive thing to speak of obedience which takes place in God himself. Obedience implies an above and a below . . . a superior and a junior and subordinate. Obedience as a possibility and actuality in God seems at once to compromise the unity and then logically the equality of divine being. Can the one God command and obey? Can the one God be above and below, the superior and the subordinate"?[8].

In the history of theology there have been two main attempts to answer these questions of Barth in the negative:

a In the subordinationism of the early Christian centuries it was maintained that if Jesus obeyed God, that was itself evidence that in his being he was less than God. Subordination in function implies inferiority in being. Under the influence of the prevailing Greek philosophy it was held that an obedient Jesus could not be truly God in the sense in which the regnant and commanding Father was God. We make two comments on this.

i We may underline the distinction between what we are saying and what was being said in that ontological subordinationism which held that in being, Jesus was less than God and was only a supreme creature, so that his obedience and humiliation were proof that, although *like* God in being (*homoiousios*), he was not identical with him (*homoousios*). Against this the Church protested that if Jesus was less than divine, then his revelation and salvation were less than divine also, his word was less than God's word and the one who came and died was not God himself but another, with all the destructive consequences of such a position that we have already outlined. It meant that in dealing with Jesus we were not dealing with God and the whole basis of the gospel was undermined at its source. Against this Arianism Athanasius declared, "But the Godhead of the Father, of the Son and of the Holy Spirit is all one, the glory equal, the majesty co-eternal", and as the whole argument of our last section established, we are agreeing with him.

What we are maintaining is a *functional* as against an *ontological* subordination. Here the whole functional element that we found inadequate when we were discussing the being of Jesus in relationship to God comes into its own. Within the one divine nature, equal and identical in Father and in Son, there is nevertheless an ability of that nature to express itself in different functions, to be first and to be second, to send and to be sent, to be glorious in the heavens and to be humble and small in the womb of Mary and on the cross of Calvary. And this humility and obedience have their whole importance and significance from the fact that they are functions of God himself, that it is a divine obedience and subordination. That he who is less than God should obey God is self-evident, but that God himself should be able and willing to humble himself and become obedient is the possibility of his incarnation and the very foundation of his grace. The early subordinationists denied the compatibility of divine being and obedience; we are speaking of an obedience that has its whole significance from the fact that it is the obedience *of* God.

ii The doctrine of God behind this ontological subordinationism is one of absolute transcendent majesty that has its roots in the prevailing philosophy. A doctrine of God that by definition excludes the divinity of the humble and obedient Son of God is obviously inadequate to the New Testament and has been imposed from outside rather than learned from within. In Philippians 2.6 for example, the fact that Christ was "in very nature God" (*en morphe theou* – there is no "although" in the Greek) is not thrown into question but rather confirmed and underlined by the fact that he did not grasp at equality with God's majesty but humbled himself and became obedient to death on a cross. The form of God (*morphe theou*) of which this passage speaks is capable of humility and obedience, of still doing in and through that humility and obedience what only God can do, of reigning and exercising divine majesty out of the humility and obedience of the cross.

So also in Matthew 11.27 ff, the Son to whom the Father has committed all things can speak with divine authority and call the weary to himself, precisely because he is meek and lowly of heart. The divine authority is confirmed, revealed and realised in the meekness and lowliness rather than being obscured and contradicted by them. The cross, the nadir of his humility, is the very place where he most exercises his divine majesty. We need a doctrine of God that will accommodate that vital New Testament truth instead of going into conflict with it; we need a doctrine of God that has been learned not in the philosophical classroom but at the foot of the cross.

b The other, less radical way, of disposing of a divine obedience and humility springs from the same sense that these things are incompatible with divinity and so has the same philosophical presupposition about the divine nature behind it. It also admits the reality of the obedience of Jesus, and its necessity to the work of atonement, but declares that it belongs to his human nature only, to his fulfilment of his historic mission as mediator and saviour, but not to his revelation of the being and nature of God.

Calvin, for example, tends to apportion the actions and attributes of Christ to alternative sources in his divine and human natures. All the attributes of majesty belong to and manifest his divinity, and all the attributes of humility belong to and manifest his humanity. Human and divine natures tend to operate rather like the man and woman in the old fashioned weatherhouse, in uneasy succession, so that when the one is on display the other is withdrawn. When Calvin speaks in this vein one begins to wonder whether divine and human natures with such opposing characteristics can credibly belong to the same real person, without tearing him apart, and his explanations are not always very reassuring.

The question, however, that we have to put to this kind of attempt to insulate Christ's obedience from his divinity is this: when Christ speaks and acts in humble obedience to his Father, is his word and action as man also the authentic word and action of God? If not, then how can we distinguish between the actions of Christ that are purely human and those which are both human and divine? And if such a central feature of Christ's action as his obedient and humble suffering and death does not belong to his action as divine Son and does not reveal the divine nature, then what does? If such reservations have to be made about the competence of his human actions to reveal and execute the divine action, what confidence can we continue to have in the humanity of Jesus as the mirror of God, and in the work of Christ as the work of God? We have to ask Calvin and those who think with him here, whether his notion of what is compatible with divine nature has been determined by what he learned somewhere else than from Christ.

Barth comments on these two attempts to keep divinity and obedience separate. Ontological subordination is impossible because "In the condescension in which God gives himself to us in Jesus Christ, he exists and speaks and acts as the One he was from all eternity and will be to all eternity. The truth and actuality of our atonement depends upon this being the case. The one who reconciles the world with God is necessarily the one God himself in his one true Godhead. Otherwise the world would not be reconciled with God"[10]. Again refusing to relate obedience exclusively to the humanity of Jesus, he says, "If God is in Christ, if what the man Jesus does is God's own work, this aspect of the self-emptying and self-humiliation of Jesus Christ as an act of obedience cannot be alien to God. But in this case we have to see here the other and inner side of the mystery of the divine nature of Christ and therefore of the nature of the one true God, that he himself is also able and free to render obedience"[11]. Writing specifically of John's gospel where these two insights are held together, and from which we have taken our bearings in this chapter, he adds, "The same Gospel of John which leaves no possible doubt about the deity of Christ in his unity with the Father, no less plainly – and with particular reference to his way of suffering and death – represents him as the One who is sent, who has a commission and who has to execute it as such, as the Son who lives to do the Father's will, to speak his words, to accomplish his work and to see his glory"[12].

If we seek to understand the nature of God in biblical rather than philosophical perspective, if, in other words, we see God not as the one decked out with a bundle of absolute attributes all beginning with omni-, but as love that has unconditional freedom to give itself and to be itself in the giving, there is no intrinsic impossibility about seeing how the same free love can express itself in Father and Son in two different ways: in the Father as initiating majesty to will the purpose of his love and the decree of his grace, in the Son the same love still doing what only God can do, but doing it in free service and obedience towards his Father. If God is indeed love, then there is nothing inconsistent in love's being free to devise and initiate, to create and to send, to command and to vindicate on the one hand, but also to serve and to be small, to descend and obey on the other. Thus the Father in heaven and the Son on earth can be one and the same God in the majesty and the humility of the same love, giving themselves in their appropriate ways to each other and to men.

If what Christ is on earth is what the Son is eternally with the Father, then we must see this functional subordination as being within the very nature of God's own life. This explains why it was the Son rather than the Father or the Spirit who became man and became obedient. It was because the humility and obedience that were manifested in incarnation were already there in the Son from all eternity. As Sir Norman Anderson puts it, "Even in the 'essential Trinity' moreover we can, I think, discern a certain element of priority and what may perhaps be termed subordination. The Bible almost always speaks in terms of a certain priority residing in, and an initiative being taken by, the Father – or simply by God . . . The very title Son suggests generation, derivation, and a certain subordination together with identity of essence . . .

It is moreover in John's Gospel – the gospel which testifies most explicitly to Jesus' claim to divine Sonship – that we find this utter dependence most consistently expressed"[13].

So also Karl Rahner asks whether, when we are thinking of the Eternal Son in his relation to the Father within the Trinity, we have to lay aside all the human characteristics of the Jesus of the gospel story (as we saw Calvin required), "May we really say without more ado that from the concept of Son of the synoptic Jesus we must eliminate his obedience to the Father, his adoration, his submission to the Father's unfathomable will? For we eliminate them when we explain this kind of behaviour in him only through the hypostatic union as such. These things are then properties of the Son, but not constitutive moments of his Sonship"[14]. It is obvious that for Rahner as for us the obedience and the submission are constitutive of the Sonship of Jesus both on earth and in heaven.

Thus he who is one in nature and being with the Father gives himself to the Father in obedience. This idea is one that is being echoed today in many quarters and has great relevance for our understanding the possibility of incarnation and the relation of humanity and divinity in Jesus. It is, however, Karl Barth who has given it magisterial exposition, so we shall let him sum it up for us. In order to humble himself and become man God "does not need to deny, let alone abandon and leave behind his Godhead to do this. He does not need to leave the work of the Reconciler in the doubtful hands of a creature. He can enter in himself, not only as the one who rules and commands in majesty, but also in his own divine person, although in a different mode of being, as the one who is obedient in humility"[15].

In the first part of this chapter we have seen that the relationship of divine Father and divine Son was the centre of all the works and ways of God in time and in eternity. The meaning of all renewal is that we should be incorporated into it so that in the Spirit we say Abba to the Father and Lord to the Son. We have seen in the second part of this chapter that the essential nature of that relationship of the Son to the Father is obedience. Obedience is not just a law given to the creature, it is the basis of the life of the Creator. That God can be low as well as high, bottom as well as top, can give as well as require is the basis of incarnation and atonement. The obedience of the Son is the means of the Father's grace and of the Church's gratitude. It binds all the children to the Father, because in obedience the first born Son went into the far country to seek and save the lost, and in the same obedience with his work done for ever and for all, came rejoicing to his Father's house.

1 H. E. W. Turner *Jesus the Christ* (Mowbrays 1976) p 94.
2 See their respective commentaries ad loc.
3 Sir Norman Anderson *The Mystery of the Incarnation* (Hodder & Stoughton 1978) p 137.
4 G. W. H. Lampe *God as Spirit* (Oxford 1977).
5 D. M. Baillie *God was in Christ* (Faber & Faber 1947).
6 C. F. D. Moule *The Origin of Christology* (Cambridge 1977) p 155.
7 John Knox *The Humanity and Divinity of Jesus Christ* (Cambridge 1967) p 106.
8 Karl Barth *Church Dogmatics* IV 1 (English translation, T. & T. Clark Edinburgh 1958) p 192.
9 Karl Barth ibid. p 195.
10 Karl Barth ibid. p 193.
11 Karl Barth ibid. p 193.
12 Karl Barth ibid. p 194.
13 Sir Norman Anderson op. cit. p 153–4.
14 Karl Rahner *The Trinity* (Burns & Oates 1970) p 62–3.
15 Karl Barth ibid. pp 203–4.

Chapter Six

The Father, the Son and the Cross

It takes the Trinity to make sense of the atonement. The interplay between Father, Son and Spirit in the relationships that distinguish and unite them is the only context within which the events of Calvary and Easter can be rightly understood. Far from being a philosophical speculation, the doctrine of God as Trinity is an implication of the Christian confrontation with the crucified and risen Jesus.

This is a connection that has come into prominence in some strands of contemporary theology, but nowhere more clearly or even startlingly than in the work of Jürgen Moltmann, especially in his seminal study, *The Crucified God*. For him everything depends on the closest mutual relationship between cross and Trinity, "What happens on the cross manifests the relationship of Jesus, the Son, to the Father and *vice versa*. The cross and its liberating effect makes possible the movement of the Spirit from the Father to us. The cross stands at the heart of the trinitarian being of God; it divides and conjoins the persons in their relationship to each other and portrays them in a specific way. For . . . the theological dimension of the death of Jesus on the cross is what happens between Jesus and the Father in the Spirit of abandonment and surrender"[1]. And again, "The doctrine of the Trinity is no . . . exorbitant and impractical speculation about God, but is nothing other than a shorter version of the passion narrative of Christ"[2]. The distinction between Father and Son comes to expression at Calvary in that the Father abandons his

Son to sin and death, whereas the Son subordinates himself in obedience to the Father. On the other hand the unity of the Godhead is affirmed when the Father raises the Son from the dead and both send forth the Spirit. "The cross of the Son divides God from God to the utmost degree of enmity and destruction. The resurrection of the Son abandoned by God unites God with God in the most intimate fellowship."[3] With this heavy stress on the doctrine of the Trinity as the theological exegesis of the event on Calvary, Moltmann can go so far as to say, "Christianity cannot therefore any longer be represented as a 'monotheistic form of belief' (Schleiermacher). Christian faith is not 'radical monotheism'. As a theology of the cross Christian theology is the end of monotheism."[4]

It will be obvious already that in Moltmann we have to do with a theologian who likes to make his points in the most extreme and paradoxical way, to make sure that we shall not miss them, but he must not be discounted for that reason. Whatever critical questions need to be asked about his general theological position, the close and detailed connection he seeks to establish between the Christian doctrine of God and the Christian doctrine of atonement is of the greatest importance for both. In this he is pointing the way forward for a theology (in the strict sense of doctrine of God) which wants to have a basic orientation to the centralities of the gospel. Following up some of his clues in our own humbler way we shall try to spell out the mutual connection between the Father/Son relationship and the events of the cross.

At the end of the last chapter we saw that the relationship of the Son to the Father was that of a divine obedience which in the life of Jesus expressed itself as a human obedience also, because it is the prototype of all obedience. We now go on to see that it is the notion of obedience which is the key to an understanding of the cross. The cross is atoning and saving precisely because on it God offers to God the obedience that is appropriate to us, out of the midst of the human situation into which he has entered wholly and with which he has identified himself completely. If obedience is the meaning of the life of Jesus, obedience is also the meaning of his death, and it is his obedience that links them together. The death of Jesus has its significance for salvation precisely because it is the death of one who has been completely obedient to his Father in every phase of his life, against all the inward and outward pressures that come against such obedience in a fallen world. His life at least from his Jordan baptism is the life of one who identifies himself with sinners, so that he lives, as it were, in the power of his death. At the same time he dies in the power of his life; what gives effectiveness and uniqueness to his death is that he dies as the one who has faced the same pressure and degree of temptation that we have to face, and yet is without sin (Hebrews 4.15). Putting the same thing positively, he has lived in such unbroken obedience to his Father, and yet in such complete identification with us, that he can offer himself as a sacrifice which is whole and unblemished and which is relevant to our situation and need.

In order to understand how this relationship of obedience between Son and Father functions for our atonement we have to summarise the situation in which the gospel sees atonement to be necessary as follows:

1 In the New Testament the human situation apart from Christ is dominated by man's personal and corporate "No" of disobedience, both to God's grace and God's command, so that he sets himself up in rebellion against God in his own claim to independence and lordship. This "No" of rebellion spoken by man to God, encounters the answering "No" of God's righteous judgement against it. God says "No" to the men who have said "No" to him. God's reaction against sin has often been described in terms of punishment. While not without its use and indeed its biblical basis, the concept of punishment, as the history of the doctrine of the atonement makes clear, is one that needs to be handled with great care. It can suggest the active imposition by God from outside of an appropriate penalty, in conformity with some scale of retributive justice, which can come to stand in unresolved tension with God's love. The New Testament often prefers to speak of God

abandoning the sinner rather than *punishing* him. It is not so much that he executes a sentence of death from above, but rather in his spurned and rejected love withdraws from the situation so that the forces of death and destruction already inherent in sinfulness and rebellion begin to operate in a more and more unrestrained way. To rebel against God is to rebel against life, and the judgement of the loving God against the sinner is that he shall be allowed to have his own way until he discovers that the rejection of life can mean nothing but death. The rebellious sinner cannot live, because he has said "No" to God's love, and therefore the living and the loving God is bound by his very nature to say the "No" of abandonment to him.

So, in Romans 1 wrath and abandonment are very closely related. "The wrath of God is being revealed from heaven against all the godlessness and wickedness of men" (1.18). When we ask how that wrath comes to expression, we have a threefold affirmation that God's wrath is God's abandonment. "Therefore God gave them over (*paredoken*) to the sinful desires of their hearts" (v.24), "God gave them over (*paredoken*) to shameful lusts" (v.26), "He gave them over (*paredoken*) to a depraved mind" (v.28). It is no coincidence that it is this key verb *paradidomi* (=to abandon, to give up), which is used again in Romans 8.32, "He who did not spare his own Son, but gave him up (*paredoken*) for us all" etc. . . . In order to do anything for those who because of sin have been given up to sin's destructive power, and lethal consequences (Romans 6.23a), the Son of God has to identify himself with them, by himself being treated as one who is abandoned and given up by God.

2　Thus what is needed in a situation thus defined as man's "No" to God in the rebellion of his sin and God's "No" to man in the abandonment of his wrath, is an obedience which will deal with both factors. It is an obedience which will (a) reverse the rebellion by replacing its "No" by a "Yes" that is spoken from the midst of very humanity which in its fallenness has uttered and been dominated by the "No" of its sin. But (b) by the same obedience the righteous "No" of God's wrath has also to be dealt with, and it can be dealt with only by being affirmed, accepted, confessed and received. That the judgement of God is borne in obedience makes the bearing a moral act; it becomes a confession of man's wrongness and God's rightness, an affirmation that the only possible end of the sinner in his rebellion is death, because only in death can the rebellious sinner and the judgement that is against him be removed. Thus on the cross Jesus interposes himself at the point of confrontation of human sin and divine wrath. Both unload themselves on to him. The sin of man comes to its climax of rebellion in its attack upon God's Son, but is countered by the "Yes" of his loving obedience to his Father, and his forgiving grace towards his enemies, enacted in the very situation sin has created. At the same time he is made sin for us (II Corinthians 5.21) so that the abandonment of the Son to death by the Father becomes the execution of God's judgement upon the sin of the world. As the Johannine Christ expresses it, "Now is the time for judgement on this world; now the prince of this world will be driven out" (John 12.31).

Thus in his obedience Jesus replaces man's "No" of rebellion by an *active* "Yes" to God's grace and God's command, and speaks it as a human "Yes" on our behalf from the midst of our humanity, so that right relationships are restored; and at the same time he speaks a *passive* "Yes" to God's judgement, by accepting it into himself in solidarity with a sinful humanity. So he gives himself to the abandonment of death in willing obedience to his Father. That is the content of the words in Gethsemane, "Not my will, but yours be done." In rendering obedience and in bearing judgement this man on behalf of all men says "Yes" to God in his death; so in the raising up of this man in the resurrection, God says "Yes" to this man who has lived and died on behalf of all men, and so to all men in him. So atonement is made between them – the "No" on both sides is turned into "Yes" through the action and passion of the life and death of Jesus whose whole virtue lies in his obedience to his Father.

3 In order to see what sort of relationship between Father and Son all this implies we can recur to Paul's statement in II Corinthians 5.18, "All this is from God, who reconciled us to himself through Christ." Firstly, the act of atonement is *from* God. Its beginning is in the *initiative* of God. Secondly, it is performed *by* God – the one who makes atonement as man and for men is himself God. Thirdly, the act of atonement is directed *towards* God. It does not have an effect only on us; it has an effect on God also, so that after it he can be said to be what he was not before it – reconciled to us.

We need an equal emphasis upon God as the source, agent, and object of atonement, if we are to keep our understanding of it in New Testament balance, so that we need to look at these three factors more closely in turn.

a Atonement is *from* God by divine initiative. The action of Christ on the cross has its primary source in the will and initiative of the Father. Where that is obscured, as in some theories of atonement traditionally most valued in evangelical circles, there can be disaster both at the doctrinal and the pastoral level. In Anselm for example God is seen primarily as the requirer of satisfaction, and in Calvin primarily as the imposer of punishment, rather than as the giver of the sacrifice. This can lead to the kind of attitude which sets the tender love of Jesus who dies for us over and against the stern judgement of the Father who requires that death. The theological consequence of such a view is to throw the unity of Father and Son in character, will and action into jeopardy, the pastoral consequence is to attack our confidence in the Father's own love for us at its heart. The result can be that we are left with a cringing guilt-ridden religion which has to hide behind the love of Jesus in order to be saved from the only just contained wrath of an angry God. This image is more fatally potent in much popular evangelical piety than we often recognise and it works untold havoc with people's ability to believe in and accept their sonship. It is good to be able to agree without qualification with Professor G.W. Lampe when in an earlier book he says about Paul's teaching here, representative of the teaching of the whole New Testament, "The initiative and the whole course of the saving work are God's. God is not a remote and unmoved judge, he reconciled us to himself through Christ, 'In Christ God was reconciling the world to himself, not reckoning to them their trespasses' (II Corinthians 5.19f) . . . In this reconciliation God is himself the prime mover, 'God commends his own love to us in that while we were yet sinners, Christ died on our behalf' (Romans 5.8). 'God having sent his own son in the likeness of sinful flesh and for sin condemned sin in the flesh . . . ' (Romans 8.3)"[5].

The classic statement of the divine origin in the Father as well as the unlimited scope of atoning love is of course John 3.16. It was the Father himself who so loved the world that he gave his Son – the love and the grace of God were not the results of atonement but its preconditions in the heart of the Father. The obedience of the Son in this supreme instance, as in all others, is subordinate response to the initiating will of the Father. That needs to be said again and again.

Even so God-centred and scriptural a theologian as Calvin can go wrong here at least in the emphasis of what he says. He speaks most easily and naturally about propitiation being offered to God by Christ, and it is only when he is expounding a text such as John 3.16 whose faithful exegesis absolutely requires it, that he balances that emphasis with a somewhat reluctant affirmation that it is God's love that provides the sacrifice, as much as it is God's righteousness that requires it. P. T. Forsyth who was in no doubt that the atonement had to be understood as propitiation of God's holiness could nevertheless say, "We put too little into God's fatherhood . . . if we think that the satisfaction of Christ was the source and cause of the Father's grace rather than its fruit"[6]. Where that is not kept in the forefront of all that we say about the atonement, the love of the Father is slandered and the confidence of the believer robbed of the central source of its assurance.

b But the agent of atonement must also be God. It must indeed be God acting as man; the one who obeys on our behalf and who suffers death for our sakes must be one of us, or else his obedience and his suffering have no relevance to us. That is why Paul can say (Romans 8.3) that he came in the likeness of sinful flesh – sharing our whole situation including all its internal and external vulnerabilities, and yet never sharing our assent to sin. He had to come as man, but the one who came as man had to be himself God. As Sir Norman Anderson puts it, "To me the very quintessence of the gospel is enshrined in the glorious affirmation, 'Herein is love, not that we loved God but that he loved us, and sent his Son to be the propitiation for our sins' (I John 4.10). But this is, self-evidently, an impossible doctrine unless one believes that there was an essential identity between the God who 'sent' and the Son who 'came'. Here the model of the Spirit of God acting in and through one who was himself a 'mere' man is manifestly inadequate; and Athanasius was surely right when he insisted that 'the Saviour must be no less than God', that 'Christ's saving work was unique, accomplished once and for all, because it was carried out by a unique person' and that 'this person' is the one eternal person of God the Son – made lower than the angels . . . so that by the grace of God he might taste death for everyone'"[7].

Our acceptance of this argument will depend upon three factors:

i   It will depend on our grasp of the incapacity of man because of sin to be the agent of his own salvation, even with the assistance of the Holy Spirit. The change required in fallen human nature, which is "dead in transgressions and sins" (Ephesians 2.1), described as new creation (II Corinthians 5.17), or new birth (John 3.7) is one of which man himself is not capable, as the very language used about it emphasises. The whole thrust of the Pauline theology is that there is no work which has its origin in man that is able to meet the requirement of God. Here the decisive deed has to be God's deed, and man features only as the beneficiary of what has been done for him by another. The more we recognise human incapacity, the more we shall see the need of divine incarnation. The attack on incarnation in modern theology is not unconnected with its deficient sense of the seriousness of sin and what it takes to deal with it.

ii To put the same point from God's side, if atonement is to be an act of grace, then it must be an act that has God himself as its agent. It throws doubt on the reality of God's grace if in the end he sent another than himself, even an inspired prophet, or a man filled with the Spirit to a pre-eminent degree, rather than coming himself. For, as we have seen, a man filled with the Holy Spirit remains in his personal being other than God so that his action can at best only point to a divine attitude, but could not as such constitute a divine action. "Thou must save and Thou alone" is a basic Christian affirmation. It is God himself who has brought about our salvation and it requires a trinitarian theology and an incarnational Christology to give that its full force and reality.

iii The New Testament represents the death of Christ as having universal and cosmic consequences, as an act to be compared in its significance only with creation itself and with the final judgement at the last day. It is the fulness of the time (Galatians 4.4) and the judgement of the world (John 12.31) which have a determining effect upon the future destiny of the cosmos and of every person in it. The cross is not seen simply in prophetic and revelatory terms – as the great window that shows us what God has always been and always will be. The cross is effective and eschatological action that reconciles the world and changes its relationship to God himself. Christ does not simply proclaim a universal truth or enunciate a universal revelation – both of which are within human capacity – he is himself in some sense a universal person, in that what he does is on behalf of all men and reverses and reconstitutes their relationship with God, in advance of their knowledge or acceptance of it. Christ's act is described as both objective and universal in the sense that it is effective as God's action for and as man quite apart from any human response to it. It has changed the universal human situation in a way with which all men will ultimately have to come to terms. The language of

Paul in II Corinthians 5 which is echoed again and again in the New Testament demands such an explanation, "We are convinced that one died for all, and therefore all died. And he died for all that those who live should no longer live for themselves but for him who died for them and was raised again" (5.14–15). "God made him who had no sin to be sin for us, so that in him we might become the righteousness of God" (5.21).

If we accept that atonement has this universal, objective and cosmic dimension, the only agent who could as man act in this eschatological and universally effective manner is God himself. If the cross and the resurrection belong with creation and the last judgement, then the only agent capable of such dimension of action is the Creator and Judge, become man in his Son to be Saviour and Reconciler once and for all for all men. Thus the seriousness of sin, the integrity of grace and the universal nature of the deed done on Calvary alike convince us that its only competent agent is God made man to do in the midst of our humanity what none but he could do.

c Atonement is *directed towards God*. The problem that it seeks to solve is not just the conversion of the sinner. Prior to that and as precondition of it, there is the removal of the divine judgement that stands against the sinner and that can be removed only by being borne. On the cross Jesus is dealing with his Father rather than with us. On our behalf he is offering the active obedience that fulfills the Father's will and the passive obedience that willingly bows to the Father's judgement against sinners, because only thus can sinful men be acceptable to God. P. T. Forsyth sees that this is the significance of Christ's silence on the cross. It is "a reticence which is only intelligible if the Son is dealing with the Father in an objective way apart from the effect of his act and agony upon us"[8]. He is suffering the abandonment that his Father's judgement decrees for sinners, he is offering the trust and obedience that alone correspond to his Father's love, and when all is over he has to commend his work into his Father's hand and await his verdict upon it in his resurrection.

The strength of so-called objective theories of the atonement is that they see that if the cross is to have the universal and creative effect claimed for it by the New Testament, it has to be a dealing with God before it is a dealing with us. Because the Father accepts this obedient man who has borne and exhausted the judgement against sin, and has done it as one of us on behalf of all of us, the Holy Spirit can be released to work out all the new births and new creations in us. It is necessary that Jesus should go away to the Father before the Paraclete can come (John 16.7). His dealing has first to be with God in order that the Spirit may, on that basis, work out a new situation in us. Our confidence in the cross is not first of all dependent on its influence upon us; rather its influence upon us depends upon the fact that quite apart from us the Son has offered a perfect obedience and offering for sin to his Father, and that in the resurrection the Father has said "Yes" to the Son, to his work, and therefore to us on whose behalf it was undertaken.

It is the divine obedience of the Son of God made available through incarnation as a relevant and saving human obedience, that has God as its source, agent and object which reconciles us. The source and the object are the Father and the agent is the Son made man for us men and our salvation. This saving enactment between Father and Son in and for our humanity, has inexhaustible effect for us and for the world. As P. T. Forsyth again puts it, the work of Christ "set up no new affection in God, but a new and creative relation on both sides of the spiritual world. It gave man a new relation to God and God a new relation, though not a new feeling to man. It did not make God our Father, but it made it possible for the Father to treat sinners as sons"[9].

4 We have been speaking of the sacrifice of obedience offered by the Son to the Father, but Moltmann reminds us of the other side of the relationship in the sacrifice of the Father in giving up his Son to death (*apodidomi*). There has been a failure to look at this side of the trinitarian transaction of the cross, partly because the biblical data are not many, but also

because of the traditional doctrine of God's impassibility, incapacity and inability to suffer, which has often made the Father seem remote and distant from the work of atonement. The only real alternative to this has been the teaching known as Patripassianism, which confused the role of the Father with that of the Son by insisting that the suffering of the Son was as such also the suffering of the Father, so that the Father was on the cross as the offerer of the sacrifice rather than in heaven as its recipient. This modalistic confusion of Father and Son has prevented what Patripassianism was trying to say from getting a hearing until quite recently.

Moltmann takes equally seriously both the identity of the Father and Son in their love and sacrifice, and yet also their difference in function as initiator and executant, as sender and sent, as giver and given. Commenting on Romans 8.32 and the Father's giving up of the Son there described he says. "In the surrender of the Son the Father also surrenders himself, though not in the same way. For Jesus suffers dying in forsakenness but not 'death' itself; for men can no longer suffer death, because suffering presupposes life. But the Father who abandons him and delivers him up suffers the death of the Son in the infinite grief of love . . . To understand what happened between Jesus and his God and Father on the cross, it is necessary to talk in trinitarian terms. The Son suffers dying, the Father suffers the death of the Son. The grief of the Father here is just as important as the death of the Son. The Fatherlessness of the Son is matched by the Sonlessness of the Father, and if God has constituted himself as the Father of Jesus Christ, then he also suffers the death of his fatherhood in the death of the Son"[10].

One wonders if Moltmann has perhaps pushed a good point too far here. One has to be very careful before one draws such extreme conclusions at a point at which the New Testament is so reticent for it explores the grief of the Father even less than the suffering of the Son. And yet we cannot but agree with Moltmann that its solitary hint is eloquent and important. We do know of the Father "who did not hold back his own Son but abandoned him, gave him up (*paredoken*) for us all". No Jew could read that without going back to Abraham on Mount Moriah preparing in great grief to sacrifice Isaac, and we may see there a picture of Abba, the God and Father of our Lord Jesus Christ, who does not this time intervene to stop the sacrifice but in divine grief lets it proceed so that his Son is abandoned to death as the representative of sinners. This is indeed the grief of the Father – a hint of what it is like to be the addressee of Jesus' cry of dereliction, and, however reticently and reverently we must speak about it, this is a constituent part of the Father's involvement in the atonement wrought by his Son.

As we have been exploring the outline of the theology of atonement, the why and the how of it, our major emphasis, until at least the last point, has been upon the action of the Son rather than upon the attitude of the Father. To redress the balance and to make a transition from Christ's unique sonship to our own derivative sonship, we cannot do better than turn to one of the most moving affirmations of God's fatherhood in the New Testament – the parable of the Prodigal Son (Luke 15.11–32).

Here it is the attitude of the father that occupies the centre of concern. The interest in the repentance of the younger son is subsidiary, for it is throughout made clear that his repentance is in no way a condition of the father's love, it is rather the necessary means by which the returning son is able to receive and benefit by that love. The father has been waiting long before the son returns and, as soon as he sees him, without enquiry about the rationale and motive of his reappearance he welcomes him with unrestrained rejoicing. The centre of the parable is its unequivocal affirmation of the Father's completely unconditional grace to sinners. As such it is Jesus' reply to the scribes and pharisees who were criticising him for showing the same kind of attitude to the same kind of people.

At first sight Jesus and the work of the cross which we have been discussing seem to have no part in this parable. The father loves freely, the son repents completely and that is enough for reconciliation and restoration, without need of sacrifice or atonement. P. T. Forsyth is very aware of this difficulty and the use his liberal critics could make of it against his own objective view of atonement and he reacts somewhat defensively, "It is not the whole fulness of the gospel that we have in that priceless parable. Christianity is the religion of redemption, and it is not redemption that we have here, only forgiveness. If it were the whole then Christ could be dispensed with in the gospel, for he is not there. And the father is not put before us as a *holy* father, but as good, patient, wise and infinitely kind . . . He stands not at all for the *cost* to a holy God of his grace, but only for the utter freeness of it"[11].

To this we would make two corrective comments. First, is it really as true as Forsyth allows that Christ "is not there" in the parable? Helmut Thielicke holds that unless Christ is very much there, the whole teaching of the parable and its presentation of the Father will collapse in incredibility and unreality. "So Jesus who tells this parable is pointing to himself, between the lines and back of every word. If this were just anyone telling us this story of the good and kindly father, we could only laugh. It is only when we see him that this father's love becomes credible. He tells us, 'He who sees me sees the Father. And what do you see when you see me? You see one who came to you down in the depths where you could never rise to the heights. You see that God "so" loved the world that he delivers me, his Son, to these depths, that to help you it cost the very agony of God, that God had to do something contrary to his own being to deal with your sin, to recognise the chasm between you and himself and yet bridge it over. All that you see when you look at me' "[12]. It is in this sense that the parable rings true of God's fatherhood only when we see that it is spoken by the Son on his way to the cross.

We have also to say to Forsyth – and of course he would not disagree with us – that there is every reason to emphasise the freeness of God's grace as well as the cost of it. Forsyth himself very pertinently remarks, "The first condition of forgiveness is not an adequate comprehension of the atonement and a due sense of the cost. That is not saving faith. Any adequate idea on that head comes only to the saved. The cross becomes a theology only by beginning as a religion. The condition of forgiveness is answering the grace and freedom of it with a like free, humble and joyful heart. It is taking the freedom of it home and not the cost. It is committing ourselves to God's self-committal to us. It is taking God at his word, at his living word, Christ – his urgent, reticent, gracious, masterful word – Christ"[13].

Many of us have known a sin-soaked guilt-ridden evangelicalism where there has been a great deal of talk about the cost of our atonement in the blood of Christ and very little upon the free and loving grace of the Father who in his intense desire for the homecoming of sinners gave his Son. The God people have been shown is the righteous judge who requires the propitiation which Jesus alone can offer, and who in response to it can just manage to restrain his wrath against us provided those redeemed by Christ continue to behave in a moral and religious way. In such a context which is of course parody, but one that many people have absorbed as gospel, the ability to answer the grace and freedom of God's forgiveness with a free and joyful heart, of which Forsyth speaks, was one that to put it mildly did not come easily, and their confidence and expectation towards God was about as great as that of a man who expected a life sentence but has been put on probation for life instead. In such a context atonement has the smell of law fulfilled rather than of grace poured out.

It was perhaps with that minimal expectation of what he could look for from his father that the prodigal came home with his modest proposal, "Make me as one of your hired servants." What wildernesses of gloomy religion lurk behind that! "I can never expect to be in your dining room, drawing room, bedroom, family circle again. Give me a little lean-to behind the cowshed – I will do every duty you prescribe and otherwise keep quiet and not draw attention to myself, provided you will just put up with me." There are some very orthodox Christians who know all about the cost of the atonement who have an attitude and expectation towards God not much better or bigger than that.

Such an attitude requires quite a different end to the story.

Let us try and concoct it. The son came home and met first his elder brother, "Is he speaking to me?" he asked anxiously. "Well he is still very upset, but if you like I will go and put in a word for you and see if that will help." After a while he returned and said, "The news is not good. He has not really got over what you have done to him, but I have pled for you, and for my sake he is prepared to let you come back on certain conditions, and provided that you cause no more trouble. He won't receive you himself and all relationships between you and him have to be conducted through me."

Something not unlike that lurks, not in the explicit teaching, but in the attitudes that are conveyed and engendered by that sort of cost-centred religion. At the best the father has been persuaded into an aloof tolerance so that the returned son is held at a distance from him, and all gratitude is due to the elder brother who has made this solution possible. Such a version of the story would go well with the attitudes of cringing passivity, inhibiting all expectation and boldness, which often result where the cost of atonement is over-emphasised at the expense of the free and unconditional grace of the Father's love to which the parable bears witness.

But of course such an ending is parody and travesty. It represents no more than perhaps the forebodings of the son on the last homeward miles with the accusations arising from his past heavy upon him. It represents perhaps the condemnation into which the Enemy would seek to bring the conscience of the Christian, so as to enervate and disqualify him from the freedom of worship and service to which God calls him. It does not in any way represent the attitude of the father in this story or that of God the Father who sent his Son into the far country to make a way home and is waiting with longing to receive us into his best blessings.

The son comes home with his request for a second-grade reception as a hired servant. What meets him is sheer unconditional grace, that reinstates him into his sonship and rejoices over him, all the more because he has been away, because there is more rejoicing in the presence of the angels of God over one sinner who repents than over ninety-nine just per-

sons who need no repentance (Luke 15.7). Into such grace
and rejoicing is the son received: "But the father said to his
servants, Quick! bring the best robe and put it on him. Put a
ring on his finger and sandals on his feet. Bring the fatted calf
and kill it. Let's have a feast and celebrate. For this son of
mine was dead and is alive again; he was lost and is found. So
they began to celebrate" (Luke 15.22–24). To be a Christian
is to believe that it is the Father who defines our identity and is
to be believed against all inner and outer accusations to the
contrary when he says to us, "This son of mine". To know that
is not to skulk in the back pew; it is to come forward with
confidence to receive the inheritance. The robe which is the
garment of sonship is accompanied by the ring which is the
insignia of authority and the sandals that distinguish the free
man from the slave. The son who comes home is invited back
into his lost inheritance, to delight again in his father's company and goodness and to rejoice.

It is this free grace that initiates the sending forth of Jesus,
and sets up the apparatus of atonement, so that when all the
cost is paid, the Father may open his arms and welcome the
many sons who are brought to glory by the only Son in whom
he reaches out to them all.

1 Jürgen Moltmann *The Crucified God* (S.C.M. 1974) pp 206–7.
2 ibid. p 152.
3 ibid. p 152.
4 ibid. p 215.
5 G. W. Lampe *Reconciliation in Christ* (Longmans 1956) pp 28–9.
6 P. T. Forsyth *God the Holy Father* (Independent Press 1957) p 24.
7 Sir Norman Anderson *The Mystery of the Incarnation* (Hodder &
   Stoughton 1978) p 125.
8 P. T. Forsyth op. cit. p 16.
9 P. T. Forsyth op. cit. p 20.
10 J. Moltmann *The Crucified God* p 243
11 P. T. Forsyth op. cit. p 8.
12 Helmut Thielicke *The Waiting Father* p 29.
13 ibid. pp 16–17.

Chapter Seven

The Father's Sons and Heirs

In John's gospel one of the immediate results of the resurrection is expressed in the risen Jesus' first words to Mary Magdalene in the garden, "Go to my brothers and tell them, 'I am returning to my Father and your Father, to my God and your God'" (20.17). The death and rising of Jesus have opened up a new relationship with God for the disciples, so that for the first time in this gospel God is said to be "Your Father" and they themselves have become "My brothers". Now that Father and Son have perfected the work of atonement, and the sacrifice of the Son has been validated by the acceptance of the Father who raised him from the dead, the family circle is open wide for others, so that new children and new brothers may be added to it.

In what remains of this book we are going to look at what our sonship means, but first we have to see that in all the positive and glorious things that are said about it, the distinction between it and the sonship of Christ is never forgotten. That is already implicit in the double phrases used to Mary, "My Father and your Father, my God and your God". "Our Father" spoken by Jesus so as to include himself and his disciples in one category never appears in the New Testament, because of course the Lord's prayer is a prayer given by the Lord for his disciples to pray together, rather than one that he himself prays with them. Within the shared sonship, the distinction between the way in which he is a Son and in which we are sons is always carefully preserved.

John does it by his use of language. Jesus alone is *huios* (son), we are always *tekna* (children). The English translations are not always consistent in the way they render these words, but in the Greek of both the gospel and the Johannine epistles the distinction is maintained (see Greek of John 1.18 and I John 3.1 where *tekna* is consistently used). The sonship of God's *tekna* consists in the fact that they receive Christ and believe in his name (John 1.12). Their right to be called his *tekna* stems not from "natural descent, human decision or a husband's will" but from the will and action of God who has brought them to himself and caused them to be born again.

Jesus the *huios* on the other hand does have a natural and essential relationship with the Father. He is *eis ton kolpon tou patros* (in the bosom of the Father) and, according to a strongly attested reading of the same verse, can even be called *monogenes theos* (only begotten God) because he partakes of the being and nature of God (John 1.18). The being of the *huios* is constitutive of the Godhead. God is God only as this Father and this Son in their relationship to one another in the Holy Spirit. He acts with God's authority because he shares God's being; with the Father he is the legitimate object of worship and, with the Father is the joint source as well as the necessary agent of creation, salvation and the coming of the Holy Spirit.

All these high claims are to be made of the *huios* but not of the *tekna*. We are not sharers of God's being, although we may be reflectors of his glory. He can be God without us as well as he can be God with us. If we will not worship him, he can raise up out of the stones fresh children who will. What binds us to him is neither a being we share with him, nor yet a need he has of us, but simply a gracious choice he has made of us. He can be God without us, but in his grace he has freely chosen *not* to be God without us, and *not* to complete his work without involving us as his chosen (but not necessary) partners in it. In the overflow of his undeserved love he has drawn us into the family, and sent his Son to live and die to bring us home. We have no right either of nature or achievement to be there, as the Son has, but in that Son he has chosen us, found us, justified us, accepted us, glorified us and made us his own for ever – all in his free mercy and grace.

The same careful distinction between Christ's sonship and ours can be confirmed if we turn from John to Paul. With Paul the distinction is not preserved by linguistic usage of such words as *huios* and *teknon*, but he has his own ways of making clear that the sonship of Jesus is of a different order from ours. He is by nature *en morphe theou* (in the form of God) according to Philippians 2.6. It is he who in the uniqueness of his resurrection is designated the Son of God with power (Romans 1.4) while we are sons through an act of *huiothesia* (adoption, son-making) which Paul always relates to the electing will of the Father on the one hand and to the finished work of Christ on the other. It is as a result of both of these, and not by any natural bond of being, that we are brought into our adopted sonship. So in Ephesians 1.5 we are told that God has "predestined us to be adopted as his sons (*prōorisas . . . eis huiothesian*) through Jesus Christ, in accordance with his pleasure and will."

Christ is not only the means of our adoption, he is the definition of all that sonship means and we were chosen in order to become like him. So Romans 8.29, "For those God foreknew, he also predestined to be reshaped into the likeness of his own Son (*summorphous tes eikonos tou huiou autou*) that he might be the firstborn among many brothers."

The same contrast between the one who is "his own Son" and those who are elected and shaped into the pattern of an already existent sonship is confirmed in Galatians 4.4–7 which is such a succinct and complete summary of Paul's teaching about the sonship of Christ and our own that I need make no excuse for setting it out once more. "When the fulness of the time came, God sent forth his own Son (*ton huion autou*), born of a woman, born under the law, that he might bring out those under the law, so that we should receive our adoption and acceptance as sons (*ten huiothesian*). Because you are sons, God has sent forth also the Spirit of his Son (*tou huiou autou*) into our hearts, crying Abba, Father. So each of you is no longer a slave, but a son, and if a son, then an heir also, through what God has done."

If we look first at what this passage says about Christ, we shall realise what a high Christology is involved in it. The coming of Christ is "the fulness of the time", the great turning point of the ages when God's final work is done. The one who is sent is the one who is already, even before he comes, God's own Son, who stands in an essential and distinct relationship to his Father. He is born of a woman into complete identification with our humanity in its lostness and condemnation, so that he may extricate us from the condemnation of the law and send upon us the Spirit who is again described in relationship to him as the Spirit of his own Son. All this describes the unique work of a unique person who stands in a unique relationship to God. It can be said of Christ alone and not of us and ultimately it will take the language of the incarnation and atonement to do justice to it.

Our sonship is of a quite different order. It is not native to us, but comes to us from him as a result of his work. We used to be slaves who were under the condemnation of the law and outside the realm of the Holy Spirit. But now as a result of God's contingent but covenant action towards us through Christ and the Holy Spirit, we have been brought out of that old set of relationships and translated into a new set. As a result of an event of sonmaking and adoption (*huiothesia*) whose objective basis is in the work of the Son, and whose subjective realisation is the activity of the Spirit, we are now able to address God as Abba and to enter into the inheritance that belongs to those who are his children.

Thus the distinction between Jesus and us needs to be carefully observed. The language of incarnation belongs to him, and the language of adoption to us, and if we try to reverse them confusion will result. To make him merely a man who has been adopted by the Spirit into a relationship of sonship with God is to confuse him with us, with all the dire consequences to our Christology that we have already discussed. To see us corporately or individually as incarnations of God is to confuse us with him, man with God, creature with

Creator in a way that the biblical tradition never countenances.

That is why it is thoroughly misleading to speak of the Church as the continuation or extension of the incarnation, as is sometimes done in Catholic circles. The incarnation of God's Son needs no continuation or extension, because it itself continues; he who united our humanity into one person with himself remains man for ever, but the nature of his union with his own humanity is different from the nature of his union with the Church. He is God and man in one person, his union with his Church is a union of many persons in one Spirit, will and life. The Church is not God's incarnate Son, but the family of his adopted sons who are the body of Christ not because he has taken them into hypostatic union with himself, but because they are one with him in the different kind of union created by the blood of the new covenant and the outpouring of the Holy Spirit, in which he abides in them and they in him in the union of faith and love which he has created.

The Church, although it is not the incarnation or its extension, is nevertheless the preliminary result and consequence of the incarnation. He took humanity that he might gather many brothers round himself as first-born. As sons with him we share his access to the Father, we have our share in his Spirit and his mission and that is why we are his brothers. But his sonship is in virtue of the divinity which he shares with the Father, whereas ours is in virtue of the new covenant which he made in his grace by becoming man and dying and rising for us. To deny the similarity is to remove him to a height of divine irrelevance where he ceases to live among us as our brother and the prototype of the new humanity. To deny the difference is to cease to honour him as our Lord and our God, and to forget our constant dependence on his undeserved grace by which alone we become and remain the adopted sons of his Father.

In the establishment and revelation of our sonship both the work of Christ and the work of the Holy Spirit have decisive parts to play. It is by the death and resurrection of Jesus that we are reconciled to the Father and made sons, so that from

being far off we become near (Ephesians 2.13). The business
of the Holy Spirit is not to make us sons, still less to make God
our Father, but rather to reveal and realise in us the sonship
that has its whole basis in the work of Christ.

"*Because you are sons*, God sent the Spirit of his Son into our
hearts, the Spirit who calls out, 'Abba, Father'" (Galatians
4.6). The role of the Spirit here is consistent with his whole
action in the New Testament. He always acts on the basis of
what Christ has already done; his work is always imitative
rather than innovative. He takes the things that are already
there for us in Christ and brings them to knowledge and
eventfulness among us. So with our sonship: there can be no
knowledge of it that is not also knowledge of Jesus Christ and
what he has done for us.

If we take the notion of sonship out of its Christological
context we shall certainly misinterpret and misunderstand it.
Apart from Christ it will be seen as something naturally and
universally true of all men, rather than as something that
depends upon the wonder of the grace of God towards sinners. Or else it will be seen as something that confers rights
("The King's kids go first class" – to which the only answer is
that there was one who didn't!), rather than something that
commits us to the kind of obedience that it meant for Jesus. It
will relapse into sentimentality and chumminess with a
heavenly Daddy who is seen as the distributor of goodies,
unless it is constantly disciplined by the humble fear of the
Lord that was at the heart of Jesus' practice of his own
Sonship. The Spirit brings us into a sonship that has its definition and normative explication not in our experience but in
the person, life and work of Jesus Christ, which our experience is to reflect as in a mirror. Secondly, it is a distinct
ministry of the Holy Spirit which makes that sonship known to
us and effective in us. God did not only send his Son to make
us sons, he sent his Spirit to let us know that we are sons of
Abba, and to enable us to live, pray and work out of the
confidence and assurance that knowledge imparts.

Not all who are sons know it or live it. Of such Christians
P. T. Forsyth says, "They treat God as power, judge, king,

providence of a sort. He is for them at most a rectorial Deity. But it is the few perhaps in their living centre and chronic movement of the soul, who experience sonship as the very tune of their heart, the fashion and livery of their will. Most Christians are not worldlings, but they are hardly sons. They are only in the position of the disciples who stood between Judaism and Pentecost, who received Christ but had not as yet the Holy Ghost. They are not sons but have only received the right to become sons. The fatherhood has not yet broken out upon them through the cross and caught them away into its universal heaven"[1].

For sonship to become "the very tune of our heart, the fashion and livery of our will" is indeed the ministry of the Holy Spirit that Paul describes in Galatians 4 and Romans 8. Just as the prodigal son in the parable came home expecting to be nothing but "one of your hired servants", there are many Christians who instead of the Spirit of sonship have "a spirit that makes you a slave again to 'fear'", who cower in the first-filled back pews of our churches because they are afraid to come further forward into their Father's house, who need to stay near the door because they have the feeling that they might need to run for it at any moment. Such may believe in theory that every Christian is called to prevailing prayer, charismatic ministry, effective witness but have no practical assurance that these things could ever happen in their own experience. Many Christians, in other words, live in constant condemnation. The Devil (Greek = *diabolos* = accuser) when he cannot trap us with wine, women and song, lives up to his name, goes all religious and throws our sins and failings in our faces, as though they had never been forgiven by Christ. He finds ways of reminding us that people who have lived as we have lived and done what we have done have no hope of all the advanced blessings that belong to God's children, and that we do very well if he can be persuaded simply to tolerate us, on account of the blood of Christ.

Dr James Packer – in a paper, not to my knowledge yet published – has proposed that we should try to understand what Pentecostals and most charismatics have called "baptism in the Holy Spirit" in terms of the doctrine of assurance. It is a suggestion that has much to commend it, because the two if not exactly identical are nevertheless very closely connected. Where there is no assurance of the relationship with the Father, there cannot either be any great expectation about the operation of the Spirit and his gifts. The Spirit has to witness to us that we are sons before he can lead us into the possessions that belong to sons (Romans 8.16–17). In terms of Luke 11.13, it is only when we can approach God as a heavenly Father who has accepted us and is willing to give his best to us, that we shall have the confidence of faith to ask him for the gift or work of the Spirit that we need. And when what might be a gift (e.g. a word of prophecy) presents itself to our minds, we shall be bold enough to speak it out only when we believe that he is Father enough to be trusted not to give us stones or scorpions, useless things or harmful things, but good gifts.

Within the charismatic renewal today, there is a good deal more talk about spiritual gifts than actual exercise of them; more discussion about the power of the Holy Spirit than actual experience of it. One of the main reasons for that is most people just do not have the confidence that God has accepted them and loves them just as they are as his children, and therefore will not let them be led astray by what is fleshly or demonic, but will give them all that he has promised – his robe, his ring, his shoes. This confidence will not be created by repeated acts of laying on of hands, but only by awareness of the Spirit's cry of Abba at the creative and motivating centres of our lives. This is what releases us from the wrong and paralysing fear of God and man that grips so many – and it is not a technique that we can master but a sovereign work of the Spirit which must liberate us.

To put the same thing in terms of the book of Acts, one result of the coming of the Spirit is that the apostles, in a situation where there is every reason to be afraid of men, are able to speak the word of God with *parrhesia* = freedom to say what needs to be said = boldness) (Acts 4.31). In the New Testament this *parrhesia* relates both to the life of prayer (Hebrews 4.16) and, as in this passage, the life of witness. We can be expectant towards God and fearless towards men, because on the basis of Christ and through the activity of the Holy Spirit, we have been convinced that God is for us so radically and completely that nobody else has any hope of standing effectively against us.

Such boldness is largely identical with that liberty (*eleutheria*) which is the trademark of the Holy Spirit in II Corinthians 3.17, and that deliverance from timidity (II Timothy 1.7) which characterise the New Testament experience of the Spirit.

The connection between assurance of sonship and freedom in the Holy Spirit is central also to Romans 8.15–17, where the entrance into the inheritance (*kleronomia*) refers back to the prior knowledge that we are sons. When the Spirit bears witness to our spirits that we are children, he also assures us that if we are children, then we are heirs – and indeed heirs of the same one of whom we are children – so, in Paul's bold phrase "heirs of God" (*kleronomoi theou*) to which he immediately gives content and particularity by the inevitable Christological reference, "joint heirs with Christ" (*sugkleronomoi Christou*). The life and power of God that we see in Christ are to be our inheritance in the Holy Spirit.

Everything that the Father gave to his one incarnate Son, he also has begun to give through him to his many adopted children. As securer, basis and giver of the inheritance Christ is unique, but as human recipient of the life, liberty, power and holiness of the Spirit, his humanity is the prototype, promise and provision of all that has still to happen in ours. The way he enters and holds the inheritance is very different from the way we enter, but the content of what we enter in our different ways is the same. The phrase "fellow heirs with Christ" comes very near defining the Christological centre of the charismatic renewal, which sees Christ as the new Adam, the ultimate man, whose new humanity spills over in the Holy Spirit to us so that we become new men and signs of the new creation (I Corinthians 15.45). For God to be our Father means that he becomes active in the Spirit to bring us into possession of the inheritance he has prepared for us in Christ.

The sons are defined by the inheritance they enter, when we know the inheritance we shall understand what it means to be a son.

There are several important points that we need to note here:

1 We have to emphasise again here what we have already hinted in chapter 2[2] that this inheritance is here defined in a Christ-centred rather than a triumphalist way, in terms of the cross and the resurrection, rather than of miracles whenever you want them and all needs satisfied. We are reminded of that precisely by the way in which Romans 8.17 ends: "Co-heirs with Christ if indeed we share in his sufferings in order that we may also share in his glory." C. B. Cranfield[3] points out that the "if" of the last clause cannot be understood as laying down conditions for entering the inheritance. The "if" is to be taken as equivalent to "in that" and the whole clause defines the inheritance. If we are joint-heirs with Christ we shall have what he had and that was suffering and glory, glory through suffering. The glory is the final thing, the ultimate content of the inheritance, and it consists of the manifestation in us of the same fulness of the power and love of God as has already been manifested in Christ especially in his resurrection. Verse 18 makes clear that the suffering along the way is for the sake of the glory and in the end will entirely yield to it, as it has done with Christ.

But to go Christ's way and to be conformed to his likeness is to reach that glory through suffering, through a participation in his cross. We in our way have to come where he came in his way, to the point in Gethsemane where the prayer that we make is not answered and has to be converted into a prayer for the doing of his will, to the experience of the silence of heaven as well as of its speech, to obedience in self-giving that has no obvious success but goes down into apparent failure, to the place where we bear faithful witness and nobody wants to know.

The continuing superficiality and immaturity of so much that passes for charismatic renewal is closely related to the fact that it seeks through all sorts of instant-answer expedients to evade that participation in the failure and suffering of Christ which is a central although not the final component of Paul's Christ-centred exposition of our inheritance in the Spirit. How can we be joint participants in what God did in Christ, if we will not take up our cross and follow him, when there is no guarantee at all of success? For although his cross is his alone in its saving efficacy, the ones that we have to carry as his witnesses are of the same shape.

2 Closely related to this is the crucial question about the *timing* of the inheritance. There is no doubt that the inheritance Paul describes in Romans 8 has to do with the last things, with God's final work of salvation; it is eschatological through and through.

But in the situation envisaged in the New Testament, that final work is in Christ both complete, present and operative, and yet at the same time hidden and not yet apparent. It is partly present and partly future, and there is no systematic way in which what can be expected now and what can only be hoped for in the future, can be set out in some tidy scheme or programme. Our adoption as sons (*huiothesia*) is from one point of view something that we have already received (8.15), but its full manifestation is still to be awaited and is described as "the redemption of our bodies" (v.23) – the final and corporal showing forth of the hidden but already hinted-at reality of our sonship. We still live largely in the realm of hope, which is related to what is not yet seen (v.24); and yet at the same time both personally and corporately we are those who "have the firstfruits of the Spirit" (v.23).

The Jewish feast of Pentecost was the thanksgiving for the first ripened fruits of the coming harvest, which were important less for themselves than for the sign and promise they gave that the rest of the harvest was soon to follow. The reason why we groan inwardly and wait (v.23) for the part of the harvest not yet gathered, is that we have received and seen enough to raise our hopes and expectations but not enough to satisfy them. What has already happened here and now in the

Spirit is a pledge and assurance of the "not yet" that still we await. Although we have already been glorified (v.30) we like the whole creation are still waiting for the glorious liberty of God's sons to be revealed.

Those who have lived through the discoveries and disappointments of the charismatic renewal will feel how exactly relevant Paul's exposition at this point is. And there is no way of resolving the tension and deciding what belongs to here and now and what to there and then. Dispensational schemes of all kinds (including charismatic ones) have tried to tidy up this situation. They have either pushed the whole inheritance on into the apocalyptic future where it has very little present relevance, or on the other hand they have made enthusiastic and unrestrained statements about what can be expected in the present. Every sick person is to be healed, every prayer is to be answered, every problem is to be solved, every gift is to be distributed – and if it does not happen lack of faith in somebody will explain the failure.

This reminds us that what is at stake here is very far from a theoretical right understanding of the balance of Bible texts or the accurate interrelation of eschatological schemes. It is rather people in deep need at central places of their lives who have called to the Lord out of their trouble and followed all the methods that have been offered to them for the building up of their faith and the reception of God's answer – and yet wonder why it has not happened as they asked. When all the explanations about the presence and absence of faith in all the parties involved have been given full weight, we have to confess that there is an area of mystery here which baffles everyone. Both extremes are obviously to be avoided. A glory that is all postponed to the future leads us into an unbelieving and fatalistic surrender to the personal, ecclesiastical or social *status quo*, and faith becomes resignation to things as they are in the assurance that in heaven or when the Lord comes it will all be different. The charismatic emphasis on a God whose lordship has begun to be exercised here and now has come as a corrective against both orthodox dispensationalism in which the kingdom is all tomorrow and a secular dismissal of any possibility of the exercise of Christ's present lordship.

But the naïve and enthusiastic proclamation that everything will happen here and now if we go about getting it the right way, owes more to the instant spirit of the age than it does to the sober realism of biblical teaching, which is all the time looking for gleams of glory but never forgets that it will have to face much suffering. Such naïve charismatic enthusiasm, because it is theologically in error, is also pastorally disastrous, as those who have had to clear up after the travelling roadshows have passed on their triumphant way very well know. There are more miracles than some evangelicals have been ready to admit, but far fewer than some charismatics on the flimsiest evidence have been too quick to claim.

When the prayer made in faith is not answered and the healing for which many have sought does not come, we are not to look for someone to accuse of failure in faith. Rather we are to remember that besides faith there is hope. Hope has to do with God's promises that are still future and hidden, just as faith has to do with God's promises that are here and now. To the person who has believed for today but has not seen the answer come today, there comes the call to hope. Hope says, "Tomorrow also is God's. Enough has happened already to assure you that the rest is on the way." The firstfruit (*aparche*) promises and bespeaks the whole harvest. God is not by any means confined by today, as if when it is over all his possibilities are over with it; he is free to act tomorrow, and at any time he chooses in all the series of tomorrows, and beyond that in the great Tomorrow when the whole inheritance is at last delivered and the sons of God at last come into their own.

In Romans 15.13 Paul characterises the Holy Spirit as the one who makes us overflow with hope. It is an emphasis that the charismatic renewal has somehow missed in its insistence on the instant, but which it very much needs to learn. "May the God of hope fill you with all joy and peace as you trust in him, so that you may overflow with hope by the power of the Holy Spirit." Between the faith that is for today and the hope that is for tomorrow and in all the groans and glory that they bring, the Christian has to live always rejoicing in the first-fruits but always longing for the harvest.

4 From Romans 8 we can trace at least in outline the *content* of the inheritance, which tells us also about what it means to be the sons who enter the inheritance. What are the great expectations of those who have come to know God as Father and themselves as his children? We shall spell that out in outline from Romans 8 now; and examine it in greater detail in the chapters that remain.

a The inheritance of God's Son, Jesus Christ, and so also of his adopted children has a cosmic dimension. It has to do with the whole creation. It is not just that we *have* the firstfruits of the Spirit in our own lives and fellowship, but rather we *are* the firstfruits of the new creation, in which God's purpose in making the world will at last be fulfilled. The frustrated creation has seen already the promise of its own liberation and restoration in the risen Christ and his renewed people so that now "the creation waits in eager expectation for the sons of God to be revealed" (8.19). In Bishop Lesslie Newbigin's words[4] the Church "is the sign, instrument and foretaste of God's kingdom" which embraces the whole reality that God has made. And when the new life of the sons of God breaks out in the Church the created world around begins to take notice and to stir in promise and expectation. To think of a personal or churchly renewal that does not spill over into a social and environmental renewal is to think smaller than God.

Paul is not really giving any comfort to the sort of emphasis on the world that was made by the secular theology of the sixties. He is certainly not saying that the Church should turn from what God is doing within it in order to give its undivided attention to what is happening in the secular world around it. He is not saying that it is that world with its concerns that writes the agenda for the Church. He is saying almost exactly the opposite, that it is the sons of God who, when they begin to come alive in the Spirit, write the agenda for the whole of creation, because the fulfilment of God's renewing purposes in the world depends on the revelation of the sons of God in the midst of it. Just as the creation was plunged into bondage when men fell, so it will break into a new springtime when man is finally put to rights. But in the meantime enough has happened for the whole creation to be standing on the tiptoes of expectation waiting to see the sons of God come into their own. The Father is also the Creator and the homecoming of his sons is a central factor in the remaking of his creation.

What Romans 8 says about this is more poetic or indeed prophetic than it is doctrinal or systematically formulated. Almost every phrase of the relevant passage has been fought over by the commentators without firm conclusion. We shall return to the theme in greater detail later. Enough has been said to show that for Paul in Romans 8 there is an incontrovertible connection between the renewal of God's sons and the restoration of all created things.

b The inheritance has to do with *prayer*. To be a son, before it means anything else, means to be in constant and intimate communication with the Father. This prayer has to be understood in a trinitarian way. It involves being caught up into the self-communication of the life of God himself. Just as the Spirit is the initiator of the life of prayer, with his cry Abba, which has its beginning and basis in the person and work of the Son, so the same Spirit is the sustainer and enabler of prayer, which without him could only plunge into perplexity and impossibility. "We do not know what we ought to pray, but the Spirit himself intercedes for us with groans that words cannot express. And he who searches our hearts knows the mind of the Spirit, for the Spirit intercedes for the saints in accordance with God's will" (v.26–27). According to these mysterious words, prayer is not simply our speaking of our own thoughts to our Father. Our words and liturgies are undergirded by and caught up into the divine litany, the Father to Son to Spirit communication that is going on in the life of God himself. "Through Christ we have access in one Spirit to the Father" (Ephesians 2.18). This mysterious trinitarian reality of the life of worship is central to our inheritance as sons.

c The inheritance has to do with eternal confidence in the Father's covenant and providing love. Paul comes back at the end of the chapter to the Father who has given us himself in his Son and therefore can be trusted to give us everything else as well (v.32). This present and providing love may be utterly trusted in the midst of accusation and condemnation, all physical deprivation, religious persecution, demonic interference, natural calamity (vv.34–39). All these things can be faced not only without fear and with detachment, but – far more – in expectation of triumph over them because the cross and resurrection of Jesus show that nothing can take us out of the power of the Father's love that has sought, saved, and secured us for ever. It is the assurance that we are loved like that, which only the Holy Spirit can give, that we need if we are to live as sons in our Father's world.

It is in this context of expectant creation, prevailing prayer and ultimate provision that we have to live out our sonship, whose beginning and end is in that Son of the Father who has been made in his manhood completely like us, and calls us in his Spirit to be completely like him, and yet who is uniquely related to the Father as the one divine Son who is the possibility and pattern of all other sonship. The Father has given him to us and us to him that we might be "shaped to the likeness of his son (*tou huiou autou*), that he might be the eldest among a large family of brothers" (v.29 NEB).

1 P. T. Forsyth *The Holy Father* p 6.
2 ibid., p 26.
3 C. B. Cranfield *The Epistle to the Romans*, Vol. 1 (T. & T. Clark 1975) ad loc.
4 In a lecture at the Fountain Trust Westminster Conference in London in August 1979.

Chapter Eight

The Will of the Father

The essence of sonship is trustful obedience – if one thing has emerged from our study, it is that. Abba is a Gethsemane word spoken by the Son made man who trusts his Father so absolutely that he can obey him completely. His call to sonship is a call to total trust and radical obedience. The sonship of the eternal Son consists of a divine obedience; the sonship of the adopted human sons of a human obedience.

Obedience so strongly stressed can sound hard and forbidding and the gospel obedience we are describing must be carefully differentiated from legal obedience. We may make several important points in this connection.

1 Gospel obedience is a response to God's grace and not its condition. The way of law says, "If you obey, God will receive you as his son"; the way of gospel says, "God has received you as his sons, just as you are in all your unworthiness. Your response to that is to obey." The returning sons are received without condition or merit, but the life of a son is lived in his Father's house and that is the place where the Father is Lord and so is obeyed. To be in God's grace is to be in his obedience, because it is our obedience that keeps us close to him and to the protection, fulfilment, provision and joy that fellowship with him brings. Gospel obedience is not constricting but liberating, because it keeps us in tune with the will of our Father which is always a will for our liberation and wholeness.

Jesus said of himself "my meat and drink is to do the will of him that sent me" – his obedience was literally the source of his renewal and refreshment. So he said to us, "If you obey my commands you will remain in my love, just as I have obeyed my Father commands and remain in his love" (John 15.10). Obedience is not a condition of being loved. Rather love has no greater gift to give us, than to put us into trustful and obedient subordination to the one who loves us, so that his love may continue to have its gracious way with us. Christ lived, died and rose in obedience to the love of his Father, and it is in abiding in such obedience that our joy will be complete. The motive is not fear of punishment but response of gratitude to grace, and the purpose is to keep us in the uninterrupted flow of that grace and to bring others there also. That is why his yoke is easy and his burden light.

2 It is an enabled obedience as much as it is a required one. The Father has given us his Son and his Spirit by whom we are able to obey him. The law as such can only impose an impossible requirement (e.g. for perfect love of God and neighbour) that proves in the end to be the law of sin and death because it leads to failure and condemnation. But "through Christ Jesus the law of the Spirit of life has set me free from the law of sin and death" (Romans 8.2). Those who walk in the Spirit are not absolved from the obligation to obey and could never ask to be, rather they are enabled again and again to fulfil it because "it is God who works in you to will and to act according to his good purpose" (Philippians 2.13).

3 It is personal obedience born in a relationship to Abba and not obedience to a code of general principles and impersonal regulations. Christian obedience is response to a person which is discerned and grasped in a community of persons, rather than conformity to a code, "Therefore I urge you, brothers, in view of God's mercy, to offer your bodies as living sacrifices, holy and pleasing to God which is your reasonable service. Do not conform any more to the pattern of this world, but be transformed by the renewing of your minds. Then you will be able to test and approve what God's will is, his good, pleasing and perfect will" (Romans 12.1–2).

This deeply personal response of self-giving in response to

God's giving of himself to us is, according to this passage, the means by which we discern, embrace and fulfil his will for us. The whole process is quite different from an attempt to conform ourselves to abstract ethical norms or that other effort – much beloved in certain Christian circles – to "apply Christian principles to everyday life" seen as the sum and substance of all sanctification.

Jesus' own obedience, as we have seen, was not at all like that. All the time he was seeking to discern what at this moment his Father was actually doing, among all the other good things that he might be doing, and to do that after him. Everything depended not upon his awareness of or ability to apply moral principles, but upon his particular sensitivity that sprang from his relationship to his Father. Of course there were constants and an overall purpose in the will of God for the mission of Jesus, that held all the details together into a coherent whole. He defines them in Luke 4.18–19. He did not, however, live by programmes or principles but by discerning from moment to moment what specific form the faithful and consistent purpose of his Father was going to take in each situation.

Our own need for guidance implied in Romans 12.1–2 does not arise from ignorance of God's general plan and purpose, but rather from our need for special insight about the Father's will in different sets of circumstances. Often our inability to find it is due to our own alienation from it, because we are conformed to the world and not conformed to the Father. It is no doubt true that God's ultimate will for all men in Christ is healing and wholeness but I shall need to know more than that when I am ministering to this particular sick person in front of me, because I need to discern as I pray how and by what steps God wants to begin to implement his will for wholeness in this person. To proclaim the general principle apart from the particular insight can lead to confusion and disappointment.

One of the positive contributions of the charismatic renewal, like other movements of spiritual revival before it, is that individuals and groups who have come alive in the Spirit begin to search with new urgency and expectation for God's guidance in every situation. They see that among all the things they might do which are in conformity to God's general will, there is one that here and now has his special *imprimatur* upon it, and there needs to be much openness to the word and prayer in the Spirit to discover what that is. There are many dangers of self-deception here, but that does not absolve us from seeking to discover still more soberly and carefully what the will of the Lord is. It was in such manner, restrained from going in one direction, and encouraged to go in another by the Spirit of Jesus (Acts 16) that Paul undertook his mission, and it is in such guided obedience that we are to undertake ours.

Such obedience, which is a response to, rather than a condition of, God's love, which is enabled as much as it is required, and which arises out of an ongoing relationship to God rather than out of abstract principles, is the obedience that we enter when we say Abba Father and it has its norm and prototype with Jesus in Gethsemane. There his sonship is not conditional on his obedience, rather it is because God is already Father who loves him and he is already Son that he can have the trust and confidence which makes his obedience possible. It is in this relationship to his Father that Jesus is strengthened for his obedience. In his agony he betakes himself to his Father to find in him the strength he needs to face Calvary, and to test again his guidance that he must indeed drink this cup – something that cannot be decided in principle but only in his grasp of the Father's will in this critical and unique situation. He discerns that will in the context of the law and the prophets, with Moses and Elijah, but at the last he receives it from his Father alone.

The central crisis that besets the charismatic renewal at the moment is that it is threatening to change this fundamental orientation towards God in obedience into a quite different and incompatible orientation towards the satisfaction of human need. The ethos of instant satisfaction is rampant in the world; the norm of self-fulfilment is the presupposition of much secular psychological counselling and social science[1]. That has had, and continues to have a distorting effect on a movement of Christian renewal that had its original impulse from an authentic work of the Holy Spirit. It is this subordination of the action of God to the need of man which constitutes the unacceptable face of the charismatic renewal, and it is becoming more and more evident on every side.

We have to be careful what we are saying here, because there is no doubt at all that for all of us much of the time it is our need that sets us running in a God-ward direction and God's grace consists precisely in the fact that he is ready to receive and deal with us on the basis of our need and to supply it. But the purpose of Jesus is never just to meet people's needs, it is always when they come with their needs, to make them disciples, to attach people to himself so that they no longer simply want to use him to get what they want for themselves, but want to follow him more than they want anything for themselves.

We can see that transition from petitioner to disciple pictured in the story of the miraculous draught of fishes in Luke 5.1–11. First Jesus satisfies the need of the frustrated fishermen for a catch. But as he does it, Peter's attention begins to turn from satisfaction in the catch, to a sense of awe and unworthiness before the power of Jesus. One of the first signs that the centrality of my need is giving way to the centrality of the person and claim of Jesus is a quickened sense of sin – in which the charismatic renewal has been strangely and persistently defective. It has spoken much more of needs that require healing than it has of sins that require repentance.

It is, however, when Peter stands before Jesus, not with a need to be satisfied, but convicted of his own sinful unworthiness and wondering if it can be forgiven, that Jesus calls Peter into discipleship, to catch men, and assures him that the power that has just met his need will be available to him as he obediently engages with Christ's calling to him. There has been a conversion from a need-based relationship to Jesus to an obedience-based relationship, and it has been accomplished through the confession and repentance of sin.

If the charismatic renewal is to continue and deepen, it must undergo such a conversion. It must cease to fabricate a distorted Christ who says, "Come and I will give you whatever

you want," and face up to the real Christ who says, "Come
and I will send you wherever I choose." It is the latter rather
than the former who is able to save us. The former can be
drawn easily into the circle of our own self-concern, which is
the very thing that most of all restricts and destroys us; the
latter calls us out of ourselves to himself. He tells us that those
who abide in him and follow him do have their needs met, not
when they are obsessed by them, but when they are seeking
God's kingdom and his righteousness. Disciples can be entrusted with whatever they ask, because what they ask will be
the things that come out of their relationship with Jesus, and
not the things that they want or need for themselves. The
renewal has surrendered in large measure to the first temptation that comes to Spirit-filled men, to use charismatic power
to make stones bread to satisfy our own needs. It needs to
learn the answer of Jesus that man does not live by having his
needs satisfied, but by obeying the word that God speaks to
him, and that when he does that, then his needs will be
satisfied as well.

The outstanding sign of the renewal's need for this fundamental reorientation towards obedience is its continued over-
concentration on healing. One has to be careful – especially if
one is reasonably healthy oneself – not to cast doubt on the
availability of Christ to all sick people. The gospels are unam-
biguously clear that he received all such with compassion and
gave himself to the service of their need. And yet he was very
well aware that healing by no means always led to discipleship, that many would fail to see their healing as the sign and
claim of the grace of God upon their lives, would simply
snatch what he did for them out of his hand and integrate it
into the unchanged context of their self-centred living. That
comes to poignant expression in the story of the ten lepers
(Luke 17.11–19) where nine took their healing and went,
because their whole link with Jesus was their need and when
the need was met, the link was broken. Only the one, when he
needed no more healing, came back to give Jesus the thanks
and praise that showed he was thinking of the Lord and not
solely of himself.

The arithmetic is still pretty realistic; healing meetings will still be thronged by the needy and the curious, but we shall still be doing well if one in ten comes back to know what the Lord requires of him by way of obedience in church, evangelism and society. The desire for miraculous healing and renewal is perhaps understandable at the beginning of life in the Spirit, but when a decade later it is still the thing to which most people mainly respond, one is left asking sad questions about what has happened to the grateful obedience of those who have been touched by the Father's grace.

If, however, it is the work of the Spirit to bring us into the likeness of Christ, what matters most is our obedience. Our renewal experiences and our spiritual gifts have significance only in so far as they are the sources or expressions of a new obedience to the Father which proves that we really are sons. Abba is a Gethsemane word – spiritual obedience is the willingness to follow Christ to the cross.

It means being ready to go on following in the absence of the signs and answers which the clamours of our own need demand. It means willingness to persevere in a dull and unresponsive church situation which can give little spiritual support or human sympathy, because we know that is where God wants us. It is to be ready to be the corn of wheat that falls into the ground and dies in seeming failure in the faith that somehow this is the way to bring forth much fruit. It is to defy our fears and reluctances and to be witnesses for Christ, in the evangelistic impact we make, in the simple lifestyle we adopt, in the responsibility for speaking and acting for Christ in the social injustices that we encounter. When the renewal produces more people who are doing that, we shall know that it has begun to find the maturity of obedience which is the only convincing proof that it knows Abba, Father.

It is my increasing conviction that the whole future of the renewal depends upon this conversion to obedience of which we have been speaking. Only so can we continue in fellowship with a Christ whose whole being was obedience. Only so can we be set free from the bondage of our own needs to the service of others. Only when we have recognised the priority of our obedience to God will we be able to tackle the problems of our subordination to human authority. The man who has humbled himself in obedience to the Father will have less difficulty in humbling himself before the legitimate authority of a brother. The leader who lives out of his obedience to God will be careful about depriving others of their liberty by bringing them into an old- or new-style hierarchical domination to himself. It is certainly true that we shall only have any real authority in the measure that we are ourselves under God's authority, and we shall only be mighty in the Spirit when with Jesus we have met with Abba in the garden and said to him very radically and realistically, "Not my will but yours be done."

In the first part of the chapter we have been discussing the practical priority of God's will over ours in his claim to obedience, but now we have to take up the much more theologically complicated question about the priority of his will to ours in grace. We give ourselves to him in obedience because he has first given himself to us in Christ. "This is love, not that we loved God but that he loved us and gave his Son to be the propitiation for our sins" (I John 4.10). First God's initiative, and then our response to it. Everyone will agree that that is the order when we are talking about the coming of Christ in incarnation and atonement. Before we moved a step towards him, while indeed our backs were turned on him, God moved towards us in his Son in sheer self-giving grace.

But when we ask about how our part and God's part are related when we are talking about the work of the Holy Spirit, the unanimity is broken. The following questions would be answered in a variety of different ways by a variety of different people. Is the action of God's Spirit in rebirth and renewal free and unconditional, or can he only act in us when we turn towards him and allow him to do so? Do I have faith because the Holy Spirit has first come and created that faith within me and given it to me, or does God's Spirit come only where he can find the faith already present in me? Does he initiate faith in us or does he issue his call and invitation and wait for us in our uninfluenced freedom to turn to him?

On the one hand there is what we can call the synergistic answer to that question. In the work of appropriating our salvation, God and man work as, in some sense, partners. Man, to be sure, cannot do his part by believing in Christ until God has first done his part in sending his Son, but equally God cannot bring the blessings of his Son and his Spirit to us until we have by our own free will opened the way for him to do it. There is a Protestant form of this synergistic teaching called Arminianism (after the seventeenth-century Dutch theologian who first propounded it) which also holds that the action of God in us is conditioned by our willingness and our faith.

Such an appeal to the free will of man as the decisive factor in whether or not we are saved appears in many Protestant evangelistic approaches. I can remember at a mass rally in Scotland in the fifties hearing Billy Graham at the climax of his appeal, saying to people, "When you come to this moment of decision, your father can't help you, your mother can't help you, your best friend can't help you and – I say it with all reverence – *God himself* can't help you." My Scottish Calvinist heart was utterly appalled, and it is so still! In the end, at the decisive point, God falls inactive and leaves it to us to save ourselves!

That kind of attitude is deeply engrained in modern Pentecostalism out of its background in Methodist holiness teaching. The baptism of the Spirit and our reception of his gifts is dependent upon our fulfilment of the conditions God lays down. If we know enough, believe enough, repent enough, pray enough, at the end we shall have them, but if not we shall not. If man fulfils the conditions, God will pour out the blessings.

In *Reflected Glory* I argued against F. D. Bruner that all teaching about Spirit baptism was not necessarily bound to this Arminian approach, and that it was perfectly possible to understand these things in the context of God's free gift of grace in Christ which is available to all, quite apart from the fulfilment of any conditions. I would still want to maintain that Bruner was in grave danger of throwing out the Pentecostal baby with the Arminian bathwater and that much renewal, in Britain at least, has indeed magnified the freeness of God's grace rather than demanded the fulfilment of human conditions.

But, having experienced the renewal longer, I would now have to agree with Bruner that there is more danger than I used to realise that the Pentecostal baby will be totally immersed in the Arminian bathwater and lost without trace. He has a real warning of what need not, but could well happen when he says, "Grace . . . appears in Pentecostalism to play a role only in the Christian's conversion, rarely appears in other discussions, and thus ceases for all practical purposes to be the centre, accompaniment and determinant of the whole Christian life. The reversal of the apostolic sequence of grace-then-obedience lies at the bottom of the Pentecostal error"[2].

We are in danger of precisely that reversal when we look for renewal not to God's free promise and grace, but to a whole series of proposed panaceas, techniques and methods which will somehow work the divine chocolate machine and make it produce the goodies we desire. In America, and to a certain extent in Britain, there has grown up a cult of charismatic gurus who offer us various simple methods which are successively guaranteed to bring us into God's blessing. The swift succession of panaceas – on average one a year – is the most eloquent testimony about their universal efficacy. We have been told that the freedom and wholeness we seek can be found in speaking in tongues, having our memories healed, praising God for everything, joining a charismatic community and sharing our lives, or – most arrogant of all – by "claiming" in faith whatever we need, whether it is a cure from cancer or the possession of a Cadillac. The picture is of a God who lays all his blessings on a table, cries out. "Come and get it – if you can!", and leaves us to work our way through the maze of right and wrong approaches with which it is all hedged around.

Of course it is significant that every one of these methods has brought blessing to some people, for each has its scriptural foundation. But with the inescapable ambiguity of all human religious enterprises, each has failed to work with many people who have come to it with at least as much faith and expectation as those for whom it did bring blessing.

The whole experience of these years makes us ask with new urgency, "How are God's promises fulfilled?" Is it by working through a catalogue of conditions and performing human works that comply with them, or is it that God in his grace leads us step by step towards the receiving of his promises at ways and times of his own choosing, so that there is no question of forcing his hand from our side? If the latter, our business in ministering to people is not to prescribe a method, but in each case to see what my Father is doing, as Jesus did, whether it be healing or waiting, bringing about a crisis or continuing a process, renewing inwardly or healing outwardly – and when we have seen what he is doing to follow him in the sovereign way he is taking. It is a delusion of the rally mentality that God has a limited three or four things he can do in people's lives, and it depends on the decision people can be induced to take whether he can do them or not.

To be more specific, let us look at the often quoted promise in Luke 11.13, "Your heavenly Father is willing to give the Holy Spirit to those who ask him." The two main elements, "his being willing" and "our asking" can be related to each other in two different ways. (a) His willing can be seen as conditioned by our asking. He is willing to give, when and as much as we ask and, if we do not ask he will not give. This is of the essence of the Arminian approach and the kind of revivalism that springs from it.

But in (b) we can see it the other way round. Our asking is conditioned by his willing. It is because he is willing that we dare and indeed are able to ask. It is the liberating creative power of his promise at work in me that gives me the liberty to ask. The Holy Spirit is not merely the gift who comes at the end of our asking, he is also there at the beginning, the creator of the desire, the strength of the seeking, the boldness of the approaching.

In both (a) and (b) there is a real human work of asking involved. In (a) it is prior to and a condition of God's willingness to give, in (b) it is the result and outworking of God's willingness to give. In the first case repentance is the condition of forgiveness, in the second it is the result of it. In the first I turn to him in order that he may forgive me, in the second I turn to him because he has already turned to me in pardon and mercy. In the first case I work at my prayer life, my believing, my purity of heart in order to reach renewal; in the second God in his grace begins by his Holy Spirit to renew me step by step into that faith, prayer, purity which are his will for me and the signs of his grace within me. It is not that he forces these things upon me against my will, but that he gives me a new freedom of heart and will, so that I am able and ready to receive them.

Theological controversy need not limit personal friendship, and I was once close friends with an Elim minister deeply committed to the Arminian alternative in this discussion, who used to get very uncomfortable if we went anywhere near the early chapters of Ephesians, because he used to claim rather quaintly that Paul was far too Calvinistic for him! I used to retort that on the contrary, it was Calvin who at least at this point was far too Pauline for him.

The Arminian gospel is concerned to require a human initiative in the appropriation of salvation, whereas Paul affirms a divine initiative in the whole process, "For he chose us in him before the creation of the world to be holy and blameless in his sight. In love he predestined us to be adopted as his sons through Jesus Christ in accordance with his pleasure and will to the praise of his glorious grace, which he has freely given us in the One he loves" (Ephesians 1.4–6).

The Arminian concern is to "challenge" a man to a response of which he is in principle capable, whereas Paul denies that we have any such capability except in so far as God restores it to us in Christ and creates it in us by his Spirit, "You were dead in trespasses and sins, in which you used to live . . . But because of his great love for us, God who is rich in mercy made us alive with Christ even when we were dead in trespasses" (2.1, 2, 4, 5).

For the Arminian, the believer has made a significant contribution to his own salvation and blessing by fulfilling the conditions and deciding to believe the promise. But for Paul, "It is by grace that you have been saved – and this not from yourselves, it is the gift of God, not by works so that no-one can boast" (Ephesians 2.8, 9). The faith through which God blesses us is itself his gift to us, and not our work that we bring to him. Arminian theology does give ground for boasting precisely where Paul says there is none . . . I am the man who in my free will fulfilled the conditions and made the decision that brought me into salvation and blessing. You can hear that kind of boasting ill-concealed on many a renewal platform, with all the scolding and accusation of others that accompanies it.

For Paul, on the other hand, the finished product, the likeness of Jesus Christ created in us by his Spirit, has its source not in the believer himself but in the God who has given it all to him, including the ability to receive it, "For we are God's workmanship created in Christ Jesus to do good works, which God prepared in advance for us to do" (2.10).

Of course in all this there is a real working out of our own salvation and a need to take due account of human responsibility and action. If our problem were one of mystic quietism we should have to emphasise that side of it. God's sovereignty is not just over man, it is in him, and when that sovereignty is exercised, man becomes a responsible active doer of good works. But we work out our own salvation only because it is God who works in us.

Our problem is the opposite, namely a man-centred renewal, pragmatic in its approach, that imagines that the laws for obtaining the divine blessing can be delivered into its hands, that when we have done our *quo* God will do his *quid*. But renewals do not come when people stir themselves to make efforts to fulfil conditions, they come when people despair of their own competence to fulfil anything, and turn to God to see what he wants to do by his grace. Renewals come not when people become frantic and have to have gifts and tongues and healings before the evening is over, but when they can be still and know that he is God and can wait trustingly and obediently for him to lead them into his promises. How sad if a renewal that was raised up to be charismatic – to magnify the grace of God and our dependence upon it – should end up in exhortations to men to adopt this method or that in a way that seeks to put God in our power rather than us in his, by depriving him of his sovereign initiative and freedom in the keeping of his own promises.

It is God that we are to trust and not our trust in God. I am in complete agreement with Professor J. B. Torrance of Aberdeen when he says, "The fallacy of legalism in all ages – perhaps this is the tendency of the human heart in all ages – is to turn God's covenant of grace into a contract – to say God will only love you or forgive you or give you the gift of the Holy Spirit *IF* . . . you fulfil prior conditions . . . But in the Bible the form of the covenant is such that the indicatives of grace are prior to the obligation of law and human obedience . . . But legalism puts it the other way round . . . The imperatives are made prior to the indicatives. The covenant has been turned into a contract, and God's grace or the gift of the Spirit made conditional on man's obedience[4].

Against that inversion we have been protesting in this chapter. The gracious will of the Father is the sole originating source of all our blessings, and all renewal and its outworkings stem from that. And yet the grace that is unconditioned by anything in us for that very reason makes a demand that is also unconditional upon our obedience. The renewal will founder if it forgets but flourish if it remembers that it is by his free grace in Christ that the heavenly Father calls us, but what he calls us into is the blessedness of an obedience that lifts us out of the bondages of our needs into the glorious liberty of the children of God.

1 For this see Paul C. Vitz *Psychology and Religion – The Cult of Self-Worship* (Lion Publishing 1979).
2 F. D. Bruner *A Theology of the Holy Spirit* (Hodder & Stoughton 1971) p 233.
3 J. B. Torrance "The Unconditional Freeness of Grace" (in *Theological Renewal* No. 9, p 11).

Chapter Nine

Our Father and our Worship

Abba is vocative; it is prayer before it is theology. There is a right theology of God's fatherhood, but the data for it are discoverable only as we actually draw near in prayer to the Father. When God is called Father in Paul and the synoptics, the context is most often prayer and worship, which is not surprising when we remember that the word Abba itself goes back to Gethsemane and the prayer life of Jesus that reached its climax there. And of course this address to the Father is central and definitive in the prayer Jesus gives to his disciples, "When you pray say, 'Father . . . '" (Luke 11.2). We must now look at the Lord's prayer not in exhaustive explanation of its meaning but to see what we can learn from the way in which Jesus invites us to approach and address his Father and ours. A few general points will prepare the way:

1 Jeremias argues convincingly that the version in Luke is likely to be nearer to the original than the one in Matthew. The Matthew form is most likely later liturgical expansion, which does not alter or go beyond the original meaning but simply makes it more explicit, as would happen naturally in the worship of the Church. The original form of the prayer behind Luke 11.2-4 was most probably "Dear Father, your name be hallowed, your kingdom come. Give us each day our daily bread. Forgive us our sins for we also forgive everyone who sins against us, and do not let us be handed over to the power of temptation." Behind the Greek *Pater* there almost certainly lies an Aramaic *Abba* which we have rendered Dear Father.

2 The Lord's prayer is related to the Jewish liturgy and in fact stands in the main tradition of Jewish prayer. Its first two petitions are closely connected with an Aramaic prayer regularly used at the end of the synagogue sermon which also seeks the hallowing of God's name and the coming of his kingdom. Jesus does not reject but takes up and enlivens the inherited liturgical forms of his people's worship. The God who is Abba can be addressed in terse liturgical formulae as well as spontaneously. The prayer Jesus gave us, far from authorising a dismissal of set liturgy, itself makes use of it and gives it new relevance and urgency in the light of the present approach of the kingdom and the king.

3 But to balance that point, the Lord's prayer is warm and familiar. Most daily Jewish prayers were in Hebrew, the special holy language of worship, but Jesus' prayer is an Aramaic, the ordinary language of the people. He prays to Abba, a God too close to be appropriately addressed in the archaic language of long ago, because he is the living God of today, deeply involved with the contemporary life of his people. As Jeremias puts it, "Jesus not only prayed in his native tongue in his private prayers, he also gave his disciples a formal prayer couched in the vernacular . . . In so doing he removes prayer from the liturgical sphere of sacred language and places it right in the midst of everyday life." Thus in the Lord's prayer the two traditions of liturgical and spontaneous prayer are reconciled at their source, and are shown to belong together rather than to be at loggerheads. It is interesting to note that a similar complementarity of the free and the liturgical in worship has been a typical discovery of many in the charismatic renewal.

4 The Lord's prayer is a particular prayer of the followers of Jesus. It was the custom for religious groups and fellowships to be identified by a distinctive form and rule of prayer. The group round John the Baptist had been so identified and the request of the disciples was that Jesus would give them a form of prayer that would arise from and express what was essential

in their life together, "Lord, teach us to pray, just as John taught his disciples" (Luke 11.1). The distinctive thing that these disciples had to learn from this master was that when they approached God they were to say Our Father.

We think of the Lord's prayer as a basic general prayer that everybody can use, neutral enough for school assemblies, useful as the prayer of the prayerless who cannot think of anything of their own to say. By such vain repetition it has been deprived of all meaning for many. For the early church it was quite different. The Lord's prayer with the Lord's supper belonged to the *missa fidelium*, the worship of the believers from which all others had been removed. It was reserved for full members and not disclosed to those outside. To pray it was among the ultimate privileges allowed only to those who were in Christ. It took *parrhesia*, Holy Spirit boldness, to dare to say Our Father. That is reflected in the introductory formula used in the liturgy of St John Chrysostom by the Orthodox to this day, "And make us worthy that we joyously and without presumption may be made bold to invoke Thee, the heavenly God and to say Our Father." It is a prayer for Christians, and only Christians are in a position to pray it, because only they know God as the Father of our Lord Jesus Christ. In that light we can now look at the various petitions.

The first petition, Your Name be hallowed, is obviously specially relevant to our subject. God's name has been uniquely revealed to be Father and in our worship the character of his fatherhood is to be glorified and proclaimed. That involves both a negative and a positive. The negative is that God's name as Father is to be guarded from all misuses and desecration. Such desecration can happen through blasphemy and bad language, but also, more subtly and dangerously, among those who have entered into the intimate and personal relationship with God to which this name invites us. God is not to be turned into an indulgent heavenly Daddy whose main function is to gratify our wishes; his authority is not to be invoked to endorse all our insights and silence our opponents. Within renewal circles there is a pious taking of God's name in vain by people who give the impression that the heavenly

Father is so busy giving them infallible messages about every detail of their lives, that you are left wondering how he can have any time left to run the universe! Their conversation is so peppered with "the Lord said" and "the Lord told me" that the whole thing degenerates into little more than charismatic garrulity, a form of words without much meaning, especially when the content of the alleged divine communication is so often entirely banal. Those who through Christ and in the power of the Spirit know his name will indeed have the freedom to rejoice in it and the fellowship it opens, but they need also the reticence, discrimination and godly fear to keep it holy.

But more positively, God's name as Father is hallowed when it is glorified and rejoiced over by his people. Speaking of the prayers of Jesus himself, Jeremias says, "It is characteristic of this new mode of prayer that it is dominated by thanksgiving . . . There is a profound reason for this . . . A fine saying from Tannaitic times runs, 'In the world to come all sacrifices will cease, but the thank-offering will remain for ever: likewise all confession will cease, but the confession of thanks will remain for ever.' Thanksgiving is one of the foremost characteristics of the new age. So when Jesus gives thanks, he is not just following custom . . . he is actualising God's reign here and now"[2].

This is consistent with Paul's use of the name Father for God. It comes characteristically in greetings and valedictions at the beginning and end of letters, and when he uses the full formula "the God and Father of our Lord Jesus Christ" (so II Corinthians 1.3, 11.31, Ephesians 1.3) it attracts to itself the exclamation *eulogetos* (Blessed be . . .). Where the living Christ is freely at work in Christian worship, there will be a priority on praise. As men full of the Spirit we shall go on addressing "one another with psalms, hymns and spiritual songs. Sing and make music in your heart to the Lord, always giving thanks to God the Father for everything in the name of our Lord Jesus Christ" (Ephesians 5.19–20). Where that voice of praise has fallen silent or given way to something else, we have ceased to hallow our Father's name. A man-centred religion will begin and end with confession and petition, with our own sins and needs in the centre. But where the centre ceases to be "Lord, bless me" and has become "Bless the Lord", when we begin to praise God for his grace, power and love as Father, as has happened in the present renewal in its best moments, then the name of the Father is being hallowed by being made first and central. In our praying amidst the Northern Ireland troubles we learned that to begin with intercession is to end with depression, but to begin with praise is to come to the point where we can ask in hope.

The first petition which invites us to praise the Father is the best preparation for the second which invites us to seek his kingdom . . . Your kingdom come. We are to seek it from him because its coming is always the work of his sovereign grace, but we are in obedience to put ourselves at his disposal so that he may work his kingdom in us, among us and through us. With the coming of the kingdom we are dealing with the last things, but with the last things that have already overtaken us in the coming of Jesus, for the coming of the kingdom is the coming of the King. The kingdom has already come with the king, it keeps on coming and giving signs and manifestations of its presence because the risen King lives and works among us by his Spirit. But its final coming, like his, is still in the future; there is still much that obscures and denies it, so that its coming has still to be sought from the Father, and the times and seasons of its final coming are the Father's secret.

That the kingdom has come gives the Christian prayer, over against the similar Jewish one, its peculiar confidence, that it keeps on coming gives it its distinctive expectation; that it will come completely as and when God decides, gives it its unique hope.

The next theme of the prayer is God's providing love for us. When we seek the kingdom and its righteousness, God will hear us about our needs and add these things to us as well. That is why in the Lord's prayer praise centred on God's name as Father precedes intercession centred on our needs, and it is the irreversible order of all right Christian worship. But if God is our Father, it follows that he will care for the legitimate needs of his people and is ready to be approached about them.

The phrase *epiousios artos*, usually rendered daily bread, has caused the commentators a lot of trouble. It can mean bread that is essential, i.e. necessary; it can mean bread for tomorrow, and it can also mean bread for the great Tomorrow, heavenly, eschatological bread. Howard Marshall declines to choose among these possibilities, "The food which God provides is food for body and soul; he gives men what they need and he gives them a rich foretaste of the rich provision available in the kingdom of God"[3]. One thinks here of John 6 as an extended exegesis of this phrase in which Jesus, as he meets the physical hunger of the multitude, offers himself to them as the bread of life which God gives to meet their ultimate hunger. One thinks also inevitably at this point of the sacrament in which these two kinds of bread become one.

The rest of this passage in Luke 11 is exegesis of this petition. Those who ask in Christ's name always receive their bread from the Father. Those who go on seeking go on finding the Father's provision for them, those who go on knocking find that the door into the Father's house keeps on opening before them. It is misleading to postulate any magical correspondence between our asking and the Father's giving. If what we ask for is bread he will give us bread, but, if he will not give us stones and serpents when we ask for bread, he will certainly not give us stones and serpents if we misguidedly ask for them. Beyond the daily bread he will give us the Holy Spirit and his gifts and fruit to be through Christ the bread for the great Tomorrow. These prayers do not move in the world of guaranteed techniques and fixed laws, but in the world of personal relationships, where prayers are changed and modified as they are brought before Father, where salutary disciplines are exercised as well as generous boons granted, and where our heavenly Father knows not only how to give what we ask but "is able to do immeasurably more than all we ask or imagine, according to his power that is at work within us" (Ephesians 3.20).

The next petition is the prayer for pardon. "Forgive us our

sins." This is the right place for it. The prayer of Jesus lends no countenance to a guilt-ridden religion that is obsessed with its sins and unworthiness. It is when we have praised the Father, exposed ourselves to the call and grace of his kingdom, set ourselves within the generosity of his provision for us, that we can and must see the wrongness of our present response to him and have recourse to his cleansing and forgiveness. Luke here translates the original debt language of the Lord's prayer (which reflects the Aramaic original which at this point Matthew retains) into sin language. The glory of God in Christ is that he forgives sins by paying the debts that they incur, and the cross of Christ, as we have seen, is the means by which he does it. It is in the power of the cross that we pray this prayer for pardon, knowing that the account can be squared because the debt has been paid.

This forgiveness has consequences; it is not simply an individualistic inner transaction with God. Forgiveness received manifests its reality in forgiveness shared. The forgiven community is also a forgiving community among its own membership and towards its enemies outside. If it is not that, it brings into doubt the reality of God's forgiveness which it exists to proclaim. The second clause reminds us of the inevitable social consequences of the gospel of forgiveness.

God's act of deliverance in Christ not only covers past transgression, but sets us free from assaulting and continuing temptation. There has been much discussion recently, in a liturgical context, whether *peirasmos* means any outward trial or inner temptation or whether it has an eschatological reference to the Trial, the great tribulation that heralds the coming of the Messiah. Marshall, with the support of most British scholarship, argues that the absence of the article is decisive against the latter meaning, so that *peirasmos* refers to "inward temptations and to outward tribulations and trials which test faith"[4]. He has a further suggestion about the meaning of "lead us not" where he takes up the point of J. Carmignac who holds that behind the perplexing Greek is an Aramaic original where to enter temptation means to fall to it and not simply to encounter it. Also the negative qualifies the entering rather than the causing, so that the whole does not mean, "Do not cause us to succumb to temptation" (with its strange implication about a God who needs to be asked that) but rather, "Cause us not to succumb to temptation," which gives a good and natural sense. It is in fact a prayer for sanctification for those who are on the way to holiness and find it strewn with many traps and allurements.

In Luke the passage in chapter 11 which begins with the Lord's prayer and continues with Jesus' further comments on some of its petitions, culminates in an invitation to pray for the Holy Spirit which the Father is willing to give to those who ask him. This is really a prayer for the empowering of all prayer. It is only in the Spirit that we can pray the Lord's prayer with any reality. Apart from the Spirit it becomes banal and boring repetition. Only in the Spirit can we call God Father (Galatians 4.6); only when filled with the Spirit can we praise his name (Ephesians 5.19), that we receive the good gifts of God (I Corinthians 12) and are convinced of sin, righteousness and judgement (John 16.8–11) and so are sanctified and kept out of the power of evil.

This prayer for the Holy Spirit does not imply the previous absence of the Spirit, any more than the prayer for the kingdom argues the previous absence of the kingdom. It does mean that he who has come is never our possession or at our disposal; the Spirit, as the very possibility of real prayer, has to be sought afresh every day from the Father. But the Father is the one who has entered into the new covenant with us in Christ and is ready continually to renew the gift of the Spirit to us, along with the life of *koinonia* with God and men that the Spirit imparts. Verse 13 is in the present tense and needs a present continuous translation to do it justice. As such it is the root of all prayer and intercourse with the Father, "Your heavenly Father goes on being willing to go on giving the Holy Spirit to those who go on asking him."

The setting of the Lord's prayer within Luke 11.1–13 has reminded us once more that even in the synoptic teaching Christian prayer is seen as at least implicity trinitarian. It is addressed to the Father, the way to whom is through Christ the Son who teaches his disciples to pray, and the possibility of that praying is the gift of the Holy Spirit. That is explicitly formulated in Ephesians 2.18, which also reminds us that such a prayer has its *locus* within the fellowship where Jews and Gentiles have through the cross been reconciled into one family. "Through him (i.e. Christ) we have access (*prosagogen*) by one Spirit to the Father."

We need to comment at greater length on this trinitarian structure of all Christian prayer.

1 Prayer is addressed to the Father – it has God the Father as its proper object. J. A. Jungmann remarks, "Looking back over the first centuries of the Christian era, we may come to this conclusion; to judge from all that survives in documents and accounts of the Church's life in this period, liturgical prayer, in regard to its form of address, keeps with considerable unanimity to the rule of turning to God (repeatedly described as the Father of Jesus Christ) through Christ the High Priest . . . It was not until the end of the fourth century that we meet by way of exception prayers to Christ the Lord, and these are not within the eucharistic celebration proper, but in the pre-Mass and in Baptism. On the other hand we know that in private prayers, both in apostolic times and later, the prayer to Christ was wellknown and customary"[5].

Here at least liturgical development reflects theological conviction. We may summarise the situation like this. Prayer and worship may legitimately be addressed to Christ and to the Holy Spirit, because they also are God, of one being and substance with the Father and therefore to be praised and adored. However, the whole movement of the life of God, both in himself and as Creator and Redeemer, has both its source and its goal in the Father. The Son and the Spirit are themselves from the Father and for the Father, so that in prayer the goal of the work of Son and Spirit is to introduce us to the Father and to establish us in fellowship with him. So, it follows from the nature of the gospel and the life of the God it reveals, that Christian prayer is properly and characteristically addressed to the Father. What it says could not be said apart from the Son and the Spirit, but what both Son and Spirit have taught it to say is Our Father.

If we do not find that right and natural, we need to ask ourselves why. There is a type of Protestant prayer that concentrates in an unhealthy way on Jesus, and that can easily become familiar and sentimental, because it has forgotten who Jesus is – the only Son of and the only way to the Father. There is a Jesuology that can lavish an all too human love on an all too human Jesus and banish God to such remote transcendence, that we are back with the idea that we have to cling to a loving Jesus to keep us right with a remote and probably angry God. There is equally a prayer that concentrates on the Holy Spirit and the gifts and blessings he can bestow in a way that forgets that these things matter only when we use them to witness to the Son and to serve the Father in a more effective obedience.

To pray *to* Jesus rather than *through* him, *to* the Spirit rather than *in* him, as the established habit of our prayer, is to betray a doubt about our relationship to the Father. The point is far from merely verbal or even theological. I have known for the first time in recent years what it means to learn from Jesus Christ that confidence in him is also confidence in his Father; this love is not only his but the love enthroned at the heart of the universe. The gospel is the gospel of the Father and spreads in its concern far beyond the personal and the churchy, to the ends of the creation and the ends of the ages. Through Christ we are related to that depth and height and breadth of love that is the Father. To forget that is to live in shrinking fear, but to rediscover the forgotten Father is the way to confidence and a far more realistic and meaningful obedience. Jesus defines the place of his Father and himself in worship in John 16.26–28, "In that day you will ask in my name. I am not saying that I will ask the Father on your behalf. No, the Father himself loves you because you have loved me and have believed that I came from God." The Father himself loves you – that is the central message of the work of Christ and therefore of the revelation of the Spirit, and we are not in the full reality of it until in prayer we are bold to approach the incandescent centre of all things and know that we are welcome and are able to say Our Father.

b Prayer is through Christ. These verses in John 16 raise the question of the nature of Christ's mediation in prayer before the Father on our behalf. There are two kinds of mediation. The first is *exclusive* – it is a going on our behalf where we shall never be able to go, so that though we are prayed for, we are still excluded. The second is *inclusive* – a going for us that results in our being able to come after, the making of a way along which we also are able to walk. It is towards this second understanding of Christ's mediation in prayer that the verses in John 16 which we quoted decisively point. "I do not say I will ask the Father on your behalf." He will not go instead of us, we are to come ourselves because the way is open. Yet it is made immediately clear that our ability to do so is entirely dependent on Christ and our relationship to him. We do not come by ourselves, but it is we ourselves who come through him. The same idea of mediation is implied in Hebrews 4.16. Because he has gone into the holiest of all as High Priest we can "approach the throne of grace with confidence".

J. A. Jungmann points out that the ancient liturgical formula with which prayer closed was "through and *with* Jesus Christ our Lord". Prayer is not what Christ does apart from us so that the Church is a place of work rather than of prayer. Prayer is not something that we do out of ourselves, a Pelagian offering of ourselves apart from him. Rather it is something we do because of him, through him and with him, so that in the Spirit direct fellowship with the Father is established and we may offer our praises, our requests, our confessions to the Father. "In that day you will no longer ask me anything. I tell you the truth, my Father will give you whatever you ask in my name" (John 16.23).

If the one Mediator between God and man exercises his mediation so as to include rather than exclude, to share access rather than to deny it, we have to make sure that that direct access to the Father is left open by the minor mediators, the ministries that God has set in his Church, which are not to stand between us and God, but are to be our helpers in coming to God. Within the renewal there is an ever present danger that we allow other people to deal with God on our behalf and to pray *instead* of us rather than *with* us. There can easily arise a notion of ministry which denies the shared access of every member of the body to the Father. A minister of healing is not someone who deals with God on my behalf, but one who stirs me up in faith so that I can be open to receive my healing not as a gift through him but as a gift from the Father to me. When eminent healers allow the adultation of others to make them forget that, they can contribute to that false notion of mediation which prevents the seekers and recipients of God's gifts from recognising and exercising their right of access to the Father.

If "Pray for me" comes to mean "Pray instead of me", go where I cannot go, where you will be heard and I shall not, it reveals a radical deficiency in Christian confidence in the person who makes such a request, and a fundamental need for that person to be radically readjusted to his relationship to the Father. "I do not say that I will pray for you; the Father himself loves you." But if "pray for me" means "pray with me" – come and support me as we have common recourse through Christ to the Father – it expresses an inclusive view of the mediating ministries of others within the fellowship of the body of Christ. When we use our different gifts and ministries to build up each other's faith, when we recognise that we never come to God in solitariness but only as members of his family, when we know that if we agree about what we ask he promises to hear us, we shall begin to exercise our shared access to the Father through the Son and in the Spirit.

5 The power and reality of prayer is in the Spirit. When Paul speaks in Ephesians 2.18 and 6.18 of praying "in the Spirit" (*en pneumati*), he is not referring either to tongue speaking or to memorable and emotional moments of prayer when the sense of God's presence was strong, although of course neither is excluded. He is defining prayer as something which in the Spirit has ceased to be a do-it-yourself activity. It is a

human activity which has its power and reality not from itself but because it has been caught up into that interflow of life between the Father and the Son which since the incarnation has taken human form and expression. To say Abba Father belongs properly to the Son of God, but he has said it in the midst of our humanity, in our place and on our behalf in Gethsemane and on the cross, so that we are redeemed by being adopted into his relationship of prayer, worship, obedience with the Father.

In the Spirit we are, of course, still ourselves. It is still we who pray our human prayers in our human thoughts and words; we are present and active, affirmed and accepted. But we have become sharers in the intercourse of Father and Son, so that we are not any more left alone to struggle Godward with our prayers, to frame our own appeal and by our own wisdom and winsomeness gain God's presence and ear, for "the Spirit helps us in our weakness. We do not know what we ought to pray but the Spirit himself intercedes for us with groans that words cannot express. And he who searches our hearts knows the mind of the Spirit, because the Spirit intercedes for the saints in accordance with God's will" (Romans 8.26–7).

In many a time of perplexity our prayer is given to us; we do not know what to formulate, we have little emotion or warmth, and yet we know that at a deeper level we are doing business with God. Sometimes a prayer in tongues can express this, and a scholar like Ernst Käsemann, who cannot be suspected of Pentecostal leanings, can argue that Paul has tongues in mind in the "groans words cannot express" of Romans 8.26[6].

However it happens, we become aware that we are not left alone with our prayer, that the intercession of Christ with his Father is not going on in some heavenly realm far above us, but in the Spirit it is going on deep within us and is being expressed through our spoken or unspeakable human prayer. Then indeed in the Spirit and through Christ we know we have access to the Father.

It was into all this that Christ initiated his disciples when he said. "When you pray, say Abba," and it is all this that in the Spirit we continue to experience and explore.

1 Joachim Jeremias *The Prayers of Jesus* (S.C.M. 1967) p 76. I am indebted to Jeremias for much of the New Testament detail in this section.
2 Joachim Jeremias ibid. p 78.
3 I. Howard Marshall *The Gospel of Luke* (Paternoster Press 1978) ad loc.
4 I. Howard Marshall ibid., p 461.
5 J. A. Jungmann *The Place of Christ in Liturgical Prayer* (Geoffrey Chapman 1965) p 164 ff.
6 Ernst Käsemann *Perspectives on Paul* (S.C.M. 1969) p 134.

Chapter Ten

In Father's World

The God who is the Father of his children is also the Creator of the world. The relationship between Father and Son, in which believers participate in the Spirit, is set within the wide horizon of God's purpose for his whole creation. We are looking here at the periphery rather than the centre of the New Testament vision, but we shall be unable to locate ourselves properly or see where we are going unless we take that universal setting more seriously than has been the habit, at least until recently, of most evangelicals and charismatics.

The direct connection between God the Father and God the Creator, although everywhere implicit in the New Testament (as for example in I Corinthians 8.6), first becomes explicit in the creeds of the Church beginning with the Apostles' Creed and its succinct statement, 'I believe in God the Father Almighty, Maker of heaven and earth." Since within the life of the Trinity it is the Father who is originator of every work, it is he who through the Son and in the Spirit is *par excellence* the Creator of all things. Thus 'God is Creator' and 'God is Father' are both essential affirmations of the scriptural gospel and of the creeds of the Church. The two statements are connected since it is the same God who is both Creator and Father, but they are not identical; to say that God is Creator is not to say he is Father or *vice versa*.

That God is related to the world as its Creator tells us that he is the responsible origin and source of all this; that he wants to be Father to his world tells us about his universal purpose in

Christ for everything that is. That he is Creator points back to the beginning from which he is working and tells us that it has all been his from the start; that he is Father points to the purpose towards which he is working and tells us that it will be his again at the end. That he is Creator tells us about his original responsibility for the world, and his continuing lordship over it; that he is Father tells us of the new relationship of response to his love into which he wants to convert all things in Christ and through the gospel. The Creator exercises his lordship in his world with the ultimate aim of drawing all men to his Son, Jesus Christ, in whom alone his fatherly love is fully expressed and revealed and of filling them with his Spirit in whom alone we relate to him as Father and respond to him as sons. In Christ God has opened the Father's house universally to all men, but not all men have come into that relationship of trust and obedience which knowing his fatherhood involves. God's fatherhood in the New Testament is never to be understood naturally as a relationship in which we all already stand, but always Christologically as something that can come to us and be received by us only in his Son.

For the Christian realisation of God's universal fatherhood is an eschatological hope which till now has been realised only in a few but presses onwards towards its realisation in all men and in the new heaven and earth which will be the home of the Father's family. We have already looked at the New Testament passages which look back to the beginning and see Christ's involvement in the original work of creation. But the connection between Christ and the whole creation also comes out in the eschatological vision of the New Testament that looks forward to the end.

In Revelation the one who sits on the throne is the Creator, "You are worthy, our Lord and God, to receive glory and honour and power, for you created all things, and by your will they were created and have their being" (4.11). But the meaning and destiny of the creation is not self-revealing and the one on the throne does not speak directly of it. It is the Lamb who has been slain who can solve the cosmic riddle and break the seals of the book of the world's destiny. "You are worthy to take the scroll and to open the seals, because you were slain and with your blood you purchased men for God . . . Then I heard every creature in heaven and on earth and under the earth and on the sea, and all that is in them singing, 'To him who sits upon the throne and to the Lamb be praise and glory and honour and power for ever and ever'" (5.9, 13).

The final dénouement has to do with all creation and is in the hands of the Lamb, so that the purpose of God as Creator and Father is to be read off from the central act of Christ's death and resurrection. In the same way in I Corinthians 15.24 Christ is said to hand over the completed kingdom to God the Father after he has put all things under his feet, so that here also the purpose of the Father to relate all things to himself is revealed and completed in his Son.

The work of Christ and of his Spirit is related not just to the inner world of personal conversions, renewals and healings, nor to the churchy world of religious communities but to the whole universe in all its physical, human and social reality. The confrontation at Calvary was with the whole world and for the whole world, the *kosmos* that God loved so much that he gave his Son for it (John 3.16). That the whole world lay in the power of the evil one became clear when the structures of Church and state, of Israel and Rome, the very powers and authorities that hold life in the world together and give it meaning, combined to crucify the Lord of glory.

This means that resurrection victory was over everything that crucified him, "Now is the judgement of this world, now shall the prince of this world be cast out" (John 12.31). The risen Lord is set to dethrone the structures of Church and state, of human society that crucified him. But he saves the created order not by destroying it but by re-creating it and bringing it into new relationship to himself and his Father. He is a healer, not an abolisher of the physical; in his resurrection his own human body is not dissolved from the physical into the psychical. His new manhood, which is the firstfruit and promise of ours, is not insubstantial vision or shapeless ectoplasm, it is *soma pneumatikon*, physical body with the structure the

Creator gave, but which now, in the power of the Holy Spirit, has passed through death and rises to a new quality of life and freedom, which is fulfilment of the old rather than its abolition. God's purpose in Christ, centred in the resurrection, is affirmative and positive in regard to his whole creation: it is "to bring all things in heaven and on earth together under one head, even Christ" (Ephesians 1.10).

Of this new creation the Church is the preliminary first-fruits. What God is doing in the Church is the preliminary sign, promise and foretaste of what he is going to do in the whole world. This is what makes the Church socially significant. The destiny of creation is seen in the risen Christ who is the *eschatos Adam* (I Corinthians 15.45), the ultimate man, who reaches the goal for which man was created, who is in right relationship to his Father, to his brethren and his enemies, to the structures and resources in his world. And when that risen Christ begins by the Spirit to be reflected in the life of his people, the Church becomes the promising sign of the new creation, as Paul saw it to be. "For God who said 'let light shine out of darkness' made his light shine in our hearts to give us the light of the knowledge of the glory of God in the face of Jesus Christ" (II Corinthians 4.6).

We need to speak soberly and realistically at this point, because there is a large part of the Church which simply reflects the structures of the world of which it is part, and is in consequence written off by that world as of no special significance. Where, however, the Church is being renewed by the Spirit into the likeness of Christ, what happens in its life has not only personal or internal importance for those involved in it, but speaks prophetically and convincingly of what God is after for his whole creation. The renewed Church is of interest, as Romans 8.22–23 makes clear, to the whole creation which is groaning and travailing in its frustration until now, but that sits up and takes notice when the sons of God within it begin to come into their own.

Paul describes this in another equally significant way in Ephesians when he says that God's present intention is that "now, through the church, the manifold wisdom of God should be made known to the rulers and authorities in the heavenly realms, according to his eternal purpose which he accomplished in Christ Jesus our Lord" (3.10–11). These "rulers and authorities in the heavenly places", often described as principalities and powers, are the religious (churches and hierarchies), intellectual (-ologies and -isms), moral (codes and customs) and political (the ruler, the market, the school, the courts, race and nation) structures that dominate and condition our lives in the world. These things were created by God in Christ (Colossians 1.16), but they rule over men who are disobedient (Ephesians 2.2), and hold them in demonic servitude (Colossians 2.20, Galatians 4.3), seeking to separate us from the love of God in Christ. Nevertheless God still uses them and urges us to subordinate ourselves to them (Romans 13.1) even though it was they who crucified the Lord of glory (I Corinthians 2.6–8) to their own undoing, for Christ has triumphed over them and disarmed them in his cross and resurrection. "Having disarmed the powers and authorities, he made a public spectacle of them, triumphing over them by the cross" (Colossians 2.15).

The Church therefore is not to be in bondage to these structures, which Christ has robbed of their demonic power, but has to show how they can be shaped by the Spirit into the different structures of the new creation. As John Howard Yoder, one of whose main theses we have been summarising in the foregoing paragraphs, puts it, "Let the Church be a restored society . . . The Church must be a sample of the kind of humanity within which, for example, economic and racial differences are surmounted. Only then will she have anything to say to the society that surrounds her about how those differences must be dealt with. Otherwise her preaching to the world a standard of reconciliation which is not her own experience will be neither honest nor effective."

This prophetic role of the Church to the whole of society is vital here. The secularist Christian misses it, because he abandons the Church, lets the world write his agenda and so is apt himself to fall captive to the demonic forces of society in one of their many forms. The individualistic Christian misses it because he has not grasped the purpose of God in Christ for the whole of creation. But the charismatic Christian with his world-affirming approach and his awareness of both the demonic and the prophetic should be among those who can catch the vision. God wants to give in local churches structures of relationship that have their roots in the central relationship to himself, but that express themselves horizontally and practically in such a way as to challenge the oppressive structures of the society in which the church lives. When the Church in the joy of its praise, in the reality of its love, in the respect for the gifts and ministries of its members, overcomes the distinctions between rich and poor, middle class and working class, educated and uneducated, black and white, it will become a relevant sign of the new creation, and will have a word of prophecy to speak that is not banal or trivial but that has power to speak to the world because it is spoken out of a way of life which is itself prophetic.

Charismatic Christians have been over concerned with the personal demonic described in the gospel stories with some bizarre results; they ought to be at least equally concerned with the social demonic of the epistles with their principalities and powers, to identify them and, in their own churches in the first place, to ask God to give signs of their overthrow and disarming. Final victory is not yet. The kingdom in its fulness will not come *in* the Church or *through* the Church. Perfectionism here as everywhere else will end in disillusion, for the Church has only the firstfruits of the kingdom, just as it has only the firstfruits of the Spirit. But it does have the firstfruits, and it can be a credible sign and prophecy of the kingdom. In its worship it can break the liturgical tyrannies of all kinds that have ceased to serve their purpose and find those that are plastic to the Spirit. It can lead its members into a new ordering of married and family life that will say more to the world than all its negative prohibitions of divorce or abortion. It can discover new forms of Christian community that are more open to the needs of single or needy people. It can pioneer economically simple ways of living that are a real expression of solidarity with the third world. It can initiate a sharing on the level of goods and possessions that speaks relevantly to the acquisitive society around. It can practise ecumenical relationships at the grassroots level that will break the log-jam at the top and will speak to the world of the possibilities of reconciliation in Christ.

It is at many of these points that renewed Christians have stopped short. Their obedience to Christ would urge them on, but their bondage to the principalities and powers of their middle-class way of life holds them and makes them afraid. They had a felt need for religious renewal which opened them to a personal experience of the Spirit, but they have no felt need for a renewal of society. Although they feel the call of God urging them forward in obedience to some of the things we have mentioned, they hold back, and renewal gets stuck at the very point where it could become locally prophetic. Churches where corporate spiritual renewal has begun get diverted into safe exercises in personal evangelism just where the Holy Spirit is calling them to become sharing communities at other levels beside the religious, which would let them say something that mattered to the watching world around. The critical question that the whole renewal faces is whether re-newed people will be led only as far as their own felt needs take them, or whether they will go on in obedience to the Father who wants to make them a sign to the world of his transforming and revolutionary power in Christ.

In Ephesians 3.14 the claim of the Father to lordship over the whole creation is specifically made, "I kneel before the Father (*Pater*) from whom the whole family (*pasa patria*) in heaven and on earth derives its name." The word *patria* is wider in meaning than the translations usually allow. It can mean family, nation, race – the real relationship structures of our created existence and it says that they have their name, that is, their meaning and significance in relation to God the Father. Notice it is not his fatherhood that takes its character from ours. His fatherhood is not ours projected into the heavens, our racial ideas expressed in transcendent and theological terms, our economic and political structures grounded in the fundamental nature of the universe.

On the contrary, all these *patriai* – structures of relationship – have been created by him who is the God and Father of our Lord Jesus Christ – and what they are meant to be begins to come to light when we live in our marriages, our homes, our work and our schools, our nation and our world in trust and obedience to the fatherhood of God as it is defined in the Son and realised in the Spirit.

It is significant that this statement about the relationship of the *patriai* to the *Pater* (Father) is set at the beginning of a prayer for renewal, as though Paul wanted to remind the Church of the cosmic context of their being strengthened with the power of the Spirit in their inward being so that Christ might dwell in their hearts through faith, and that with all the saints they might grasp, not just for themselves but for their whole society and world, all the dimensions of the love of God in Christ (Ephesians 3.14–16).

Thus the Father's will in Christ extends to the renewal of everything he has made, to the transformation of creation to be the home of his transformed humanity, the rescue of the created structures of life from the demonic powers that control them, so that the *patriai* become vehicles for the mutuality of love and order that we see in the *Pater* and his Son. Just as the fall of the first Adam meant the bondage and frustration of creation in all its life, so the manifestation of the last Adam will mean the liberation of creation in all its life. Of that the local church, in its members and its structures, in its own reflection of the love of Father and Son in the Spirit, is to be prophecy and sign that will challenge and confront its part of the world.

We dare not quite stop with that general conclusion, which would be a bit too much like going to heaven on the last note. the *patria* of Ephesians 3.15 has a wide meaning but it also means fatherhood, and it reminds us that the fatherhood of God is to be reflected very practically and specifically in the kind of fathers that we are in our own families. Amidst all the highflown talk about principalities and powers and the relationship structures of society, it is good to remember that the first such structure, where Jesus lived as Son of his Father and exercised his renewing ministry, was the home of Mary and Joseph at Nazareth into which he was born and where he grew towards his great mission. One of the results promised to Zechariah in connection with the great renewal which God was about to inaugurate through the Baptist was that he would "turn the hearts of the fathers to their children" (Luke 1.17). Many of us who are Christian ministers, when we remember the time we have given to others compared with the time we have given our own families, will read these words with shame.

But there is no escaping from this particular implication which the whole logic of the argument of this book forces upon us. If there is one place where the relationship of the divine Father and the divine Son is to be reflected it is at the point where parents and children live together in our own families. There is good scriptural warrant for holding that if a man cannot be a good father in his own house, he is unlikely to be a good minister in Christ's Church (I Timothy 3.4–5).

Within our family circles there needs to be that functional subordination of younger to older, of second to first, of son to Father that we saw was characteristic of the life of God himself as revealed in Christ. There is so little sense of obedience in our lives, so little sense of order in our society, because our homes have ceased to become that place of learning obedience and discipline that they were meant to be. The exhortations in the epistles for sons to obey their fathers are not simply socially conditioned but have their firm Christological basis in the subordination of Christ to his Father. This is the order that God has established for our life because it is the order of his own life.

But, to prevent that from being understood in some legalist, fundamentalist way, as tends to happen in much charismatic writing about the family, we have to remember that the obedience of the Son is always response to the love and grace of the Father, that the Son obeys the Father because he can trust his love for him. That is why the instructions in Ephesians and Colossians make clear their specifically Christian orientation by including not only exhortations to sons to obey their fathers, but exhortations to fathers to love their sons (Ephesians 6.4, Colossians 3.21). For the heavenly Father loves and cherishes his Son, gives himself to him and seeks his glory, grieves over his loss of him, and joys to raise him from the dead. Jesus had security and courage and could obey because he knew that he stood safe and secure in the love of his Father.

There has been a great abdication of fatherhood in our society, as part of the collapse of all the structures of authority. There is no easy way back. The only authority that has an intrinsic right to be obeyed is the authority of a great love for our children that will express and commend to them the greater love of the heavenly Father. We should be over them, only so that we can serve them and lead them to that day when their relative loyalty to us will have led them past itself to an absolute obedience to the one they have to love and serve before us. To hear the young Jesus declare, "I must be about my Father's business," was a blow for Joseph, but it was also his justification. He had fulfilled his fatherhood by commending through it the fatherhood of God and by then taking second place to it.

Jesus' great submission to God was learnt first in the little submissions to his parents and, even when the claim of God meant his leaving them, it never meant even for him the abnegation or dissolution of the lesser claim. He went back, the young man from the temple, and was submissive to his parents (Luke 2.51) and, if John is to be followed, he made provision for his mother among the company of his disciples at the very moment when he was at the climax of his obedience to his heavenly Father.

Some of us need to be liberated from our parents to be free for God; some of us need to have regard to the claims of our parents as part of the claim of God. Some of us need to make good use of the few years in which it is possible to be the mirrors of the fatherhood of God to our children, so that through the love and order of our homes, they may know his love and the obedience to which he calls them.

If there is to be true order in Church and state, there must be true order in our homes, where fathers and sons, parents and children together, as the promise and first sign of what is in store for the whole creation, learn to say Abba to the God and Father of our Lord Jesus Christ, and to trust and obey him as his sons.

Postscript

We have covered a great deal of ground in this book, perhaps too summarily really to satisfy. I should, however, in conclusion like to register three main convictions that were central when I started and have been reinforced as I have continued.

1 The Holy Spirit is telling those of us who in recent years have spoken most of renewal that the renewal we have so far espoused has been far too small. It has often been far too naïvely over-simple in its claims, and unready to face and think its way through difficulties. There are those who think that renewal has nothing to do with theology and will find too much theology in this book. They have to learn that there is no such thing as a renewal without a theology but only a renewal with a bad theology or a renewal with a good one.

   I have tried to suggest that the right theology for renewal is not a testimony-based teaching about experiences and gifts, but the classical trinitarian theology that has its roots in the New Testament and that centres in the incarnation, death and resurrection of the only Son of the Father as the focal point of all creation and recreation. I suggest that unless we see our renewal in that context it will remain far too small.

2 There is in this book a central stress on God's fatherhood as implying our obedience – more perhaps on the side of absolute demand than of ultimate succour, although I hope I have shown that the former makes no sense except in relation to the

latter. But this emphasis is deliberate. A need-centred renewal will not be able to go further than the needs that prompted it. In my view, the present renewal is hampered and hindered because many involved in it have not been converted from need to obedience, from satisfying themselves to being at God's disposal. The call to sanctification has been lost in the promises of gifts and healings and blessings. I believe that until the call to obedience is heard and heeded we shall be left with the disillusionment that cheap grace always brings in its train. When it is heeded we shall have a renewal that in depth, outreach and maturity will go far beyond anything we have seen so far.

3   I believe that at the heart of all this there is a great simplicity. The theology of trinity, incarnation, atonement, of the purpose of God in society and family is only the map. Without the map the car will lose its way, but there is no motion in the map, no transforming power in a theology of fatherhood and sonship. The simplicity of the work of the Holy Spirit is to cry Abba in our hearts, and to bring us the grace that will transform us into trust and obedience. This book has been written out of my own discovery of Abba which has been just as transforming, if less dramatic, than the earlier renewing experience of the Spirit itself, and that has begun to turn me in some of the new directions indicated in this book. I believe that in the Spirit and through Christ we are being called back from all charismatic onesidedness to the forgotten Father to find something of the wholeness of our life in him. My prayer is that some of what has been written here may bring some of its readers to the point where in wonder and simplicity we hear the Spirit himself speaking in our hearts and saying Abba, Dear Father.

Index